KT-484-731

LONDON RECORD SOCIETY
PUBLICATIONS

VOLUME XXIV
FOR THE YEAR 1987

Dedicated to the memory of Virgil Pozzini

RICHARD HUTTON'S COMPLAINTS BOOK

The Notebook of the Steward of the Quaker Workhouse at Clerkenwell, 1711–1737

EDITED BY

TIMOTHY V. HITCHCOCK

LONDON RECORD SOCIETY
1987

© *London Record Society, 1987*
SBN 90095224 5

Phototypeset by
Wyvern Typesetting Ltd, Bristol
Printed and bound in Great Britain at
The Bath Press, Avon

CONTENTS

ABBREVIATIONS   vi

INTRODUCTION   vii

RICHARD HUTTON'S COMPLAINTS BOOK   1

ADDITIONAL DOCUMENTS   96

INDEX   103

LONDON RECORD SOCIETY: PUBLICATIONS   109

ABBREVIATIONS

DNB	*Dictionary of National Biography*
FSSWA	Archive of the Friends' School, Saffron Walden, Essex
GLRO	Greater London Record Office
Hitchcock	'The English Workhouse, a Study in Institutional Poor Relief in Selected Counties, 1696–1750' (Oxford Univ. D. Phil. thesis, 1985)
HLRO	House of Lords Record Office
SFL	Society of Friends' Library, Friends' House, London NW1
SPCK	Society for Promoting Christian Knowledge

INTRODUCTION

The Quaker Workhouse at Clerkenwell was one of the most radical experiments in co-operativism made in the eighteenth century. 'Richard Hutton's Complaints Book' is the personal notebook of this institution's fourth and most successful steward. Hutton was steward of the Quaker workhouse from 1711 to 1737, and used this notebook to record events in both his life and the life of the institution he managed. The complaints book was not a personal diary nor was it a letter book, it was rather Richard Hutton's general notebook, wherein he would complain and speculate, record compliments and note insults. Through it Hutton has given us a view into the internal workings and problems of an eighteenth-century institution.

Richard Hutton
Very little is known about Hutton's life prior to his arrival at Clerkenwell. He was never an important individual, and would interest historians very little were it not for his association with the Quaker workhouse. But he was an exemplar of his type, of, that is, the eighteenth-century bureaucrat; he was one of the faceless men who managed the thousands of institutions established by both private charity and local government.[1] He was born in Lancaster to a Quaker family in 1662 and trained as a tailor. By 1702 he was living in Lombard Street in London and was married to Sarah Steed. In the next ten years he and Sarah moved first to Clements Lane, then Pudding Lane and finally to the workhouse at Clerkenwell. In all, they had nine children all of whom died in the first year and a half of life. Richard died in 1737 at the age of 65 of an apoplectic fit and was buried at Bunhill Fields.[2]

The complaints book shows Richard Hutton to have been an excellent administrator. He combined exactness and probity with charity and flexibility. He also, however, possessed a high regard for his own worth, was easily insulted by threats to his authority and was deeply concerned for his reputation. He appears in many ways to have been a rather difficult and cold man. Nowhere in this book does he mention the loss of his and Sarah's last child in 1717.[3] But there are a few items which show

1. By 1777 there were 1,916 parochial and borough workhouses alone in England: HLRO, 'Poor Rate Returns, 1777', Parchment Collection, Box 162.
2. SFL: 'London & Middlesex Marriages 1657–1719', i; 'L. & Mdx. Births, 1644–1719', i; 'L & Mdx. Burials, 1700–1749', i.
3. Richard Hutton's son, Richard, died at the age of 18 days in November 1717. The existence of a child is mentioned by William Townsend (**85**), but the death of this, the Hutton's ninth and last child, is not mentioned by Richard himself. SFL, 'L. & Mdx. Births, 1644–1719', i; 'L. & Mdx. Burials, 1700–1749', i.

another side of his character. He had a deep concern for the poor and for children and was extremely careful to record any evidence of their gratitude to him (**57, 58**). There is no evidence that he possessed a sense of proportion about the problems he faced; he seems to have been incapable of seeing the humour that pervades many of the scenes he describes. But he certainly did possess a sense of charity, one which he was able to maintain despite receiving rough treatment at the hands of those to whom it was directed.

As steward of the workhouse, Hutton had a wide range of duties. Any problem arising was naturally his affair and responsibility. At the same time, however, he worked under immense constraint. He was answerable first to the workhouse committee, made up of elected representatives of the six monthly meetings supporting poor people in the house,[4] second, to the poor themselves, who when dissatisfied had frequent opportunities to make trouble both inside and outside the house, and third, to the broader community upon which the workhouse depended for legacies and work, and whose opinion Hutton was made aware of in letters and complaints (**66, 143**). Hutton's struggle to overcome these constraints is fully recorded in his complaints book and his qualified success in doing so is likewise apparent.

John Bellers and the history of the Corporations of the Poor
The workhouse Hutton managed was established in 1702 as the direct result of the writings and efforts of the early eighteenth century's most humanitarian and radical thinker, John Bellers.[5] Before going on to discuss Hutton's role in the house and its history under his stewardship, we must first look at Bellers' and the Quaker workhouse's place in a broader history of workhouse care for the poor and English radicalism.

John Bellers' writings had a profound influence on nineteenth-century co-operativism and communism. Karl Marx acknowledged his debt to him, describing Bellers as a 'veritable phenomenon in the history of political economy'.[6] Likewise, Francis Place and Robert Owen were

---

4. Quaker administration in London was performed by a series of meetings. At the top of the organisation was the Yearly Meeting, and below that the regional Quarterly and Six Weeks Meeting, and finally the six local Monthly Meetings. There were also, however, several special organisations with specific responsibilities for poor relief. First, there was the Meeting of Twelve, made up of two representatives from each of the Monthly Meetings, which had established a flax-spinning scheme in 1677. Second, there was the Women's Meetings, which were considered to have special responsibility for the poor, though their role was never defined. Third, there was the workhouse committee, composed of three representatives from each of the Monthly Meetings, which had direct responsibility for the institution at Clerkenwell. These were the main meetings concerned with administration in London, though there was a plethora of others which were primarily devotional. See William C. Braithwaite, *The Second Period of Quakerism* (2nd edn., York, 1979), 251–8, 272, 275–8; Arnold Lloyd, *Quaker Social History, 1669–1738* (London, 1950), 33.
5. Lloyd, 47n.; A. Ruth Fry, *John Bellers, 1654–1725. Quaker, Economist and Social Reformer* (London, 1935), 7–8.
6. Quoted in Braithwaite, *Second Period*, 571.

deeply influenced by Bellers' ideas.[7] But, despite his later importance, Bellers has been largely ignored by historians. He is discussed in the Quaker historiography,[8] and the Institute for Workers Control did reprint his pamphlet, *Proposals for Raising a Colledge of Industry*, in 1980;[9] but writings on British radicalism have tended to ignore the particular forms the communist and co-operative traditions of this country took in the first half of the eighteenth century, and in the process have neglected to include Bellers in their hagiography and, more particularly, the Quaker workhouse in their list of co-operative experiments.

Bellers published his *Proposals for Raising a Colledge of Industry* in 1696. In it he suggested that 'It's in the interest of the rich to take care of the poor, and their education, by which they will take care of their own heirs . . .: For . . . is there any poor now, that some of their ancestors have not been rich? Or any rich now, that some of their ancestors have not been poor?'[10] He also baldly stated a labour theory of value, suggesting that his college '. . . will make labour and not money, the standard to value all necessaries by.'[11] Further, he pointed out the dependence of the rich on the poor; he asked, 'if one had a hundred thousand acres of land, and as many pounds in money, and as many cattle, without a labourer, what would the rich man be, but a labourer?'[12]

The college Bellers proposed was in fact a small economic commonwealth, a wholly independent co-operative community in which no money would be needed, all middlemen eliminated, and to which each member would contribute according to his ability; taking, in turn, according to his needs. The pamphlet describes the college as a mixed agricultural and manufacturing settlement wherein three hundred people, two hundred of them being labourers and craftsmen, would live. The organisation was to be highly paternalistic, only people contributing more than £100 to the foundation being allowed to vote in making by-laws and in choosing officers, and was expected to produce large profits from an early date. There were to be discipline and rules, but no corporal punishment.

Bellers describes the advantages of living in his college for the poor. They were to enjoy 'all things needful in health or sickness, single or married, wife and children; and if parents die, their children well educated and preserved from misery, and their marrying encouraged, which is now generally discouraged'. They were to be relieved from the constant competition of a capitalist economy – 'instead of every body endeavouring to get from him, every body is working for him . . .' And finally, 'as they grow in years in the college, they may be allowed to abate an hour in the day of their work, and when come to sixty years old (if merit prefer them not sooner) they may be made overseers; which for ease and pleasant life, will equal what the hoards of a private purse can

---

7. For information on Bellers' influence on later radicals see *The First Worker Co-operators, Proposals for Raising a Colledge of Industry, by John Bellers* (Nottingham, Institute for Workers Control pamphlet no. 68, n.d., *c.* 1980), 3–4.
8. See for example, Lloyd, 40; Fry, *Bellers*; Braithwaite, *Second Period*, 571–94.
9. *First Worker Co-operators*.
10. Ibid. 12.   11. Ibid. 13.   12. Ibid. 12–13.

give; and excel, in so much as it has less care and danger of losing.'[13]

Bellers did not develop his ideas in isolation. He was both the product of a long-standing tradition, and an active member of a group of social policy reformers. In terms of his intellectual antecedents the most obvious and direct lines of influence came from the Quaker community, which had been relieving its own poor since the 1650s. Quaker relief had always been generous and well thought out; each monthly meeting was responsible for its own paupers, and an emphasis was always placed on self-help.[14] But more than this, Quaker practice spawned several proposals and experiments in poor relief which were reflected in elements of Bellers' ideas. One early poor-relief proposal was that addressed to Parliament by Thomas Lawson in 1660. Lawson argued that each parish should employ an 'undertaker' to arrange with manufacturers for the employment of paupers and to relieve those unable to work. He also wanted to establish an employment exchange, and suggested that 'none be put to service until they be first taught to spin, knit, sew, [or] learn some trade or way of livelihood'.[15] Similarly, in 1669 George Fox advised Quakers to set up 'a house or houses wherein an hundred may have rooms to work in, and shops of all sorts of things to sell, and where widows and young women might work and live'.[16]

Neither of these proposals was ever put into practice, but Bellers himself was involved with at least one Quaker experiment which did reach fruition. In 1680 he became the financial adviser to a scheme based in London designed to employ the poor in spinning flax, which had been started in 1677 by the Six Weeks Meeting. One hundred pounds was raised and used to buy a stock of flax, which was then given to the Quaker poor to spin up at home or in prison.[17]

The elements in both George Fox's proposal and the London flax-spinning scheme suggesting that the poor should be provided with the means to work for their own benefit reflect a humanity towards and trust in the poor that must have been influential in Bellers' intellectual development. However, these sorts of ideas were in no way restricted to the Quaker community, nor was Bellers reluctant to involve himself in non-Quaker experiments.

Poor-relief proposals made a century before Bellers formulated his ideas display elements that are familiar from his writings. At the beginning of the seventeenth century, for instance, Rowland Vaughan in his *Most Approved and Long Experienced Water-Works* advocated the establishment of a huge, co-operative, agricultural and manufacturing colony.[18] However, the seventeenth-century tradition on which Bellers

13. Ibid. 20–1.
14. William C. Braithwaite, *The Beginnings of Quakerism to 1660* (2nd edn., York, 1981), 143; Lloyd, 32.
15. Quoted in Braithwaite, *Second Period*, 559.
16. Ibid. 571.
17. Stephen Macfarlane, 'Social Policy and the Poor in the Later Seventeenth Century' in A. L. Beier and Roger Finlay, eds., *The Making of the Metropolis, London 1500–1700* (London, 1986), 259; Lloyd, 40.
18. Rowland Vaughan, *Most Approved and Long Experienced Water-Works* (London, 1610).

drew reached its highpoint in the writings of Samuel Hartlib and the foundation of the Corporation of the Poor of London in the Interregnum. Hartlib had advocated and established a workhouse for London's poor, which provided both training for the young and capital in the form of stock for the poor to work up at home. Hartlib's experiment incorporated both a large degree of humanity, and the expectation that the labour of the poor could be harnessed for their benefit.[19] The full force of Hartlib's influence would later be felt by the founders of the Corporations of the Poor, among whom Bellers must be counted.

Another influence on Bellers' work and ideas was Thomas Firmin, who holds the middle ground between the Interregnum and the 1690s. Firmin had established his scheme for employing the poor in the 1670s, and through it provided the poor with training and capital.[20] In its organisation and ends Firmin's scheme was precisely similar to the London flax-spinning establishment in which Bellers was involved, and later, in the 1690s, both men were closely associated with the London Corporation of the Poor, Bellers as an assistant and Firmin through his nephew, Jonathan James.[21]

None of the experiments and proposals described above was as consistently humanitarian and co-operative as Bellers' College of Industry, but in them can be seen fragments of Bellers' economic analysis and humanitarian impulse towards the poor. They all shared with Bellers a fundamental belief in the real value of the labour of the poor, and a commitment to their humane and kindly treatment. Similarly, in some of the proposals, particularly those by Rowland Vaughan and George Fox, one can see a belief in the desirability of a co-operative organisation of labour.

If Bellers had been alone in his advocacy of a co-operative and humanitarian provision for the poor, or if he and his contemporaries in the same tradition had failed to put their ideas into practice, he would deserve little more than a footnote. But he was not alone, he was part of a much wider intellectual movement in the 1690s and 1700s, and neither he, nor his contemporaries, failed to use their ideas as the basis for practical experiments.

The ideas of Vaughan, Hartlib and Firmin, described above, did not influence Bellers alone, but had an equally strong influence on a whole generation of writers on social policy, an influence which resulted in

19. See S[amuel] H[artlib], *London's Charity Inlarged, Stilling the Orphans Cry* (London, 1650); [Samuel Hartlib], *A Designe for Plentie, by an Universal Planting of Fruit-Trees* (London, 1653); Samuel Hartlib, *Considerations Tending to the Happy Accomplishment of England's Reformation in Church and State* (London, 1647); Samuel Hartlib, *A Further Discoverie of the Office of Publick Address for Accommodations* (London, 1648); Valerie Pearl, 'Puritans and Poor Relief: The London Workhouse, 1649–1660' in D. Pennington and Keith Thomas, eds., *Puritans and Revolutionaries* (Oxford, 1978), 206–232.

20. For material on Thomas Firmin and his relief project see H. W. Stephenson, 'Thomas Firmin, 1632–1697' (Oxford Univ. D.Phil. thesis, 1966); Macfarlane, 'Social Policy', 259–60; A. G. Craig, 'The Movement for the Reformation of Manners, 1688–1715' (Edinburgh Univ. Ph.D. thesis, 1980), 98–9; Thomas Firmin, *Some Proposals for the Imployment of the Poor* (London, 1681).

21. Macfarlane, 'Social Policy', 262.

analyses of the problem of poor relief very similar to Bellers' own. In the writings of John Cary, Robert Clayton and even John Locke an emphasis on the value of the labour of the poor, humanity and co-operativism can be seen. It was these men, and their less literary fellows, who founded fourteen Corporations of the Poor between 1696 and 1711,[22] and who contributed to four failed attempts to reform the old Poor Law in line with their ideas.[23]

In the later 1690s two connected circles of men developed, one centred on the Board of Trade and the other on the Corporation of the Poor in London. In 1695 John Cary had written his *Essay on the State of England in Relation to its Trade* which incorporated a proposal for the establishment of Corporations of the Poor, large workhouse schemes wherein the labour of the poor would be harnessed to finance the venture, and wherein the poor would have the best treatment available – the old looked after and the young educated.[24] As a result of Cary's efforts the Bristol Corporation of the Poor was established in 1696 by Act of Parliament[25] and thirteen similar institutions set up in the following 15 years.

One of the Corporations established on Bristol's model was that at London, and it was with this institution that Bellers was associated. He was among the 52 assistants first elected to govern the Corporation, and in his capacity as an assistant we can assume he came into contact with men like Jonathan James and Robert Clayton, and through them with the ideas being formulated by the Board of Trade between 1698 and 1701.[26]

The Board of Trade spent years analysing the problem of poverty and formulating possible solutions. It took evidence from Thomas Firmin and John Cary, and three of its members, John Locke, John Pollexfen and Abraham Hill, each presented separate proposals for the reform of the Poor Law which incorporated the idea of setting up institutions wherein the poor would care for the less fortunate among their number according to their ability, and wherein the labour of the poor, which it was assumed would be highly remunerative, would be used to support the institutions created.[27] These proposals were then incorporated into Parliamentary bills.[28] Anthony Hammond, Rowland Gwynne and Humphrey Mackworth each in turn, armed with the Board's proposals, presented bills to Parliament, which were read and reread, passed to the Lords and brought back, but which never became law. Through these bills and reports,

---

22. For a list of these institutions see T. V. Hitchcock, 'The English Workhouse, a Study in Institutional Poor Relief in Selected Counties, 1696–1750' (Oxford Univ. D.Phil. thesis, 1985; cited hereafter as Hitchcock), 14n.
23. Hitchcock, 22–39.
24. John Cary, *An Essay on the State of England in Relation to its Trade* (Bristol, 1695), 150–9.
25. E. E. Butcher (ed.), *Bristol Corporation of the Poor, Selected Records, 1696–1834* (Bristol Record Society, iii, 1932), 1.
26. Macfarlane, 'Social Policy', 262.
27. See Hitchcock, 25–8.
28. Hitchcock, 28–39.

however, the ideas they incorporated were popularised, and local experiments, already set on foot by John Cary, were encouraged.[29]

The debt the Corporations of the Poor owed to Samuel Hartlib and Thomas Firmin was large. The very organisation of these institutions was modelled on the workhouse establishment by Hartlib and described in the 1662 Act of Settlement,[30] and Firmin was extremely active in influencing both the Board of Trade through the evidence he gave to it, and the Corporation of the Poor of London through his association with many of its elected assistants. Indeed, the London Corporation at first attempted simply to provide stock and training for the poor in the same way Firmin had done for the previous 20 years.[31]

Perhaps because both the founders of the Corporations of the Poor and Bellers shared many of the same intellectual antecedents, but also because they moved in the same circles, there is a great similarity between Bellers' ideas and those expressed in the organisation and running of the Corporations of the Poor. Bellers' ideas, which at first seem isolated in a period populated by repressive workhouse schemes, on closer examination come to appear merely the purest and most sophisticated representative of a whole series of workhouse proposals.

The Corporations of the Poor did contain houses of correction, and were empowered virtually to imprison paupers and to inflict brutal physical punishments on the recalcitrant,[32] but their design likewise incorporated two aspects of the tradition in English poor relief central to Bellers' own scheme. First, just as Bellers believed the labourers and handicraftsmen housed in his college would come to form a caring community, helping one another rather than competing, the advocates of the Corporations expected the inmates to form a 'workhouse family', wherein the healthy would take care of the sick and a separate workhouse identity would develop.[33] More than this, inherent in the idea of a workhouse family was that of a common purpose among the inmates, a belief that each inmate would work hard for the benefit of the whole workhouse community.

Second, the Corporations were designed to provide the best possible care for the poor. Good food, healthy conditions and a regular life were to be given the inmates as their desert either at the end of a long working life, or, as in the case of the young, as an insurance for the well-being of future generations.[34] This was not the age of 'less eligibility' or the

---

29. Rowland Gwynne's bill, though it did not become law, did result in the publication of several pamphlets, including John Cary, *Reasons For Passing the Bill for Relieving and Employing the Poor of the Kingdom Humbly Offered* (London, 1700); John Cary, *Proposal Offered to the Committee of the Honourable House of Commons* (London, 1700) and M.D., *A Present Remedy for the Poor: or the Most Probable Means to Provide Well for the Poor* (London, 1700).
30. 13 & 14 Chas. II c.12.
31. Macfarlane, 'Social Policy', 262.
32. For a detailed description of the powers of the Corporations of the Poor, see Hitchcock, 17–22.
33. For example see M.D., *A Present Remedy for the Poor*, 11–12.
34. See John Cary, *An Account of the Proceedings of the Corporation of Bristol* (London, 1700), 9–17.

workhouse test, rather it was a period of increasing sympathy towards the poor.

It would be wrong to see the foundation of the Corporations as a result of purely humanitarian impulses; they incorporated many repressive and cruel elements, but at the same time, with the Quaker Workhouse at Clerkenwell, they were a result of a long tradition of English humanitarian and co-operative poor relief, which was extreme in its belief in the necessity and virtue of treating the poor with kindness and humanity. Bellers' ideas and institution still stand out against this background, but not because they contained anything new, rather because they did not contain the repressive aspects of other proposals.

The Clerkenwell Workhouse

The institution Hutton managed was founded in 1702. It housed and cared for about a hundred poor elderly people and children, who were supported in the house by the Monthly Meeting to which they belonged, each meeting paying between 12d. and 3s. per week for each inmate.[35] The building the institution occupied had been built in 1662 as a workhouse for the Corporation of the Poor of the County of Middlesex, probably at the instigation of Sir Matthew Hale.[36] It remained a workhouse only until 1672, but continued to serve as the site of a poor relief establishment for most of the rest of the century.[37] The London Quakers took over its lease from Sir Thomas Rowe, who had used it for his College of Infants founded in 1686, and in doing so gained access to half the building, the other half being used throughout this period as a county house of correction.[38]

The building was situated at the corner of Corporation Lane and Bridewell Walk and is shown on John Rocque's 1747 map of London. It enclosed a large square, and was surrounded by relatively open countryside. That half of the structure leased by the Quakers included 46 rooms, 31 of which were fitted up as lodging rooms, ranging in size from 8 ft. by 10 ft. to 20 ft. by 85 ft. Of these rooms most were used to accommodate the elderly, with one, two or three people occupying each room, while three rooms were used as dormitories for the children. Besides these, there were also cellars, kitchens, a parlour, several

35. There are three items entirely devoted to the Quaker Workhouse at Clerkenwell available in published form: David W. Bolam, *Unbroken Community: The Story of the Friends' School, Saffron Walden, 1702–1952* (Cambridge, 1952); *Memoir of John Sharp, Late Superintendent of Croydon School* (London, 1857), and [Timothy Bevan], *An Account of the Rise, Progress and Present State of the School and Work-house Maintain'd by the People called Quakers, at Clerkenwell, London* (London, 1746).
36. See E. G. Dowdell, 'The Economic Administration of Middlesex from the Accession of Charles II to the Death of George II' (bound typescript deposited at the Greater London Council History Library), 46–66.
37. For a number of years in the 1670s the building was used as a prison, and in 1686 it was taken over by Sir Thomas Rowe as the site of his College of Infants, in which use it continued until Rowe's death in 1696. See Dowdell, op. cit., 66–9, 84–95; Braithwaite, *Second Period*, 585.
38. Dowdell, 'Economic Administration of Middlesex', 50, 64n.; David W. Bolam, *Unbroken Community*, 19.

storerooms and workrooms, a stable and a brewhouse. It was a commodious and airy building, ideally suited to the use to which it was put.[39]

Having published his *Proposals for Raising a Colledge of Industry* in 1696, Bellers presented it to the Quaker Yearly Meeting in London in 1697, which in turn recommended it to the Monthly and Quarterly Meetings around the country.[40] It was not immediately taken up, but in 1698 the Six Weeks Meeting in London commissioned a report on Quaker poverty, concluding that the Quaker communities of London and its neighbourhood contained '184 aged people most of them capable of some work and 47 children or more, most them fit to put to some kind of business',[41] and that the establishment of a college of industry was practical. Originally, the London Monthly Meetings, which made up the Six Weeks Meeting, believed they needed an Act of Parliament on the lines of those passed for the establishment of Corporations of the Poor in order to set up such an institution, but after petitioning Parliament and consulting legal counsel this was deemed unnecessary.[42] The sum of £1888 was raised, the lease taken and necessary repairs carried out on the building.[43]

The government of the house was strongly paternalistic and highly organised. A committee was established, made up of three members from each of the six Monthly Meetings in London, which met regularly and had control over all aspects of the administration of the house. John Bellers proposed a bill of fare and a system of rates was decided upon (**150**). Once the house was established a steward was chosen. George Barr was given the post in 1702 and paid a salary of £20 a year, 'he to be supplied with all necessaries except the furniture of one room and his own apparel'.[44] While the workhouse committee determined questions of policy and sat in judgement over disputes arising in the house, it was the steward who made sure the institution worked. Although his role and powers were never precisely defined it fell to him to see that orders were obeyed, that food was bought and served, the inmates properly clothed, that the accounts were kept accurately, and perhaps most importantly that the goods produced by the inmates were made economically and sold at a profit. In most respects the role of the steward was determined by the personality of the man holding the post. Whether he was independent or insecure seems to have determined the number of times he felt obliged to appeal to the workhouse committee on questions arising from the day-to-day administration of the workhouse. Hutton, for example, seems to have been quite timorous in his dealings with the workhouse committee for at least the first few years of his administration. He appealed to it over

---

39. R. Hyde (ed.), *The A to Z of Georgian London* (London Topographical Society publication no. 126, 1982), 4. For a list of all the rooms, their dimensions and the uses to which they were put see FSSWA, 'Standing Minute Book of the Committee of the Quaker Workhouse at Clerkenwell, 1701–1792', pp. 25–6.
40. Fry, *Bellers*, 7.
41. Quoted in *Memoir of John Sharp*, 4.
42. Lloyd, 47n.; Fry, *Bellers*, 8.
43. *Memoir of John Sharp*, 5.
44. FSSWA, 'Best Minutes, 1701–1708', ff. 24, 25.

matters of internal discipline of a kind that do not seem to have arisen or at least were not reported during the tenure of his predecessors.

At its first foundation 32 elderly friends entered the house, and gradually, after that, the house's population was expanded, the 'ancient friends' being followed by children and finally in 1707 by paying residents and 'scholars'.[45] At first both the elderly and children were encouraged to work, the elderly being provided with materials to practise their own trades, which included winding silk, picking oakum, spinning thread and cotton, sewing, carding and shoemaking, while the children were either employed about the house or set to spinning mop yarn.[46] But the amount of work done was gradually restricted, and by the 1710s only the children were required to contribute to their own support, the elderly being enjoined merely to 'lend a helping hand to each other'.[47]

The first ten years of the house's existence were characterised by bad management and confusion. Three stewards came and went between 1702 and 1711, and at least one of them left bad debts to the house when he resigned.[48] Likewise, the manufactures of the workhouse were found to be unremunerative. In 1710 it was reported that the inmates earned less than 1d. per week per person.[49] Nevertheless, the commitment to the house on the part of the Monthly Meetings continued, and its role gradually changed in order to fit most easily within the affordable needs of the Quaker community. The education of children gradually came to take up more of the resources of the house, and in 1706 children began to be accepted into the house from all over the country.[50]

By the beginning of the 1710s the house was obviously in decline. It received fewer legacies than it had at first, and while the Monthly Meetings willingly took care of the day-to-day expenses, capital investment remained unprovided for. In 1711 Richard Hutton took up the post of steward,[51] and it was Hutton who turned the house around, striving to create an efficient and inexpensive management and ensuring that money came in both from the sale of goods produced and from legacies. The gradual change of emphasis from housing and employing the poor to the education of children was partially a result of Hutton's endeavours. But, as Hutton's notes demonstrate, he did not manage his part in this transformation without difficulty. The house was always in the public eye, and that public did not hesitate to pass judgement on it and Hutton's management (**66, 143**). In the complaints book, Hutton records how

45. FSSWA, 'Best Minutes, 1701–1708', f. 125.
46. For a list of trades being practised by inmates in 1704 see ibid., f. 1.
47. FSSWA, 'Standing Minute Book of the Committee of the Quaker Workhouse at Clerkenwell, 1701–1792', p. 95.
48. Samuel Trafford, Hutton's immediate predecessor, was discharged in 1711 for having 'very misapplied the cash put into his hands for the necessary use of the house', and Trafford's predecessor, John Powell, left the house owing four shillings, which debt was 'thought something dubious': FSSWA, 'Best Minutes, 1708–1714', ff. 79–80, 99. Hutton's predecessors were George Barr, 1702–4, John Powell, 1704–9, and Samuel Trafford, 1709–11. See FSSWA, 'Best Minutes, 1701–1708', ff. 25, 62; FSSWA, 'Best Minutes, 1708–1714', ff. 44, 97, 99.
49. FSSWA, 'Best Minutes, 1708–1714', ff. 79–80.
50. FSSWA, 'Best Minutes, 1701–1708', f. 92.
51. FSSWA, 'Best Minutes, 1708–1714', f. 97.

Quakers and non-Quakers alike confronted him with what he deemed to be spurious complaints based on the garbled reports of those opposed to the house (**99, 105, 106, 141, 145, 148**). At one point he received an anonymous letter from a non-Quaker complaining that, 'This day I was informed that the children under your care have not a sufficient allowance of food to fill their bellies . . . I am sorry that such a report should be raised among your people for I did think you always took the best of care amongst your poor. Children are hungry and growing and require more food, but hungry bellies and cold water betwixt meals do not agree, and raising them at five a clock in the morning and making them work without their clothes is very hard for children to bear' (**66**). This complaint was unfounded, but caused Hutton great concern nonetheless. In several places Hutton also suggests that there was a large body of Quakers who were actively opposed to the very idea of a Quaker workhouse, and who worked for its demise (**99, 141, 145**).

But Hutton's most serious problems arose not from external sources, but from the residents themselves. The workhouse population was made up of an extremely varied group of individuals. Besides the problems naturally associated with housing and educating children and adolescents (**8, 42, 67, 113, 130, 145, 147**), Hutton faced the difficulty of moderating between and satisfying the house's two types of adult residents, the poor and the fee-paying inmates. The pauper inmates of the house, who were supported by the Monthly Meetings, expected to be and for the most part seem to have been treated with a large degree of sympathy and for-bearance. But as Hutton suggests in 1717, the pauper residents also expected all the money available for the house to be expended upon them. Complaints about the diet of the house, in particular, were extremely common. The poor believed they should receive the immedi-ate benefit of any legacies left to the house. Hutton recorded these complaints thus: 'when our family heard . . . [that several bequests had been left to the house] I was told by some of them and in a very untoward and reflecting manner, saying, we hear that the house begins to save money by the poor, also said, that friends gave not their money to the house with that intent but it was in order that it might be laid out upon the poor to comfort them, and not to be hoard up' (**141**). This sort of expectation naturally led to conflict between those most interested in the long-term future of the institution and those seeking immediate gratifica-tion in the form of better conditions or diet. These complaints from the poor were a reflection of how they saw their relationship to the house, and likewise, of the extent to which the house represented a pure humani-tarian and co-operative tradition. Hutton could not see the house's money as other than a trust for the future. He was faced with a problem posed by the success of any co-operative venture: to what extent can the profits of the work of temporary members of the organisation be kept aside for the benefit of future generations? In any co-operative with a high turnover there is always a temptation for those in control during a period of prosperity to view extraordinary profits as a windfall, and to use them for their own benefit exclusively. Because the Quaker workhouse was paternalistic in its management this view could be ignored, but the arguments of the poor reflect an expectation that they as individuals had a strong claim on any funds available, and in turn a degree of control over the management of the house. Hutton overcame this problem primarily by appealing to higher authorities – the workhouse committee and the Monthly Meetings who supported the inmates (**99, 141, 148**). It was more difficult for him to do this when confronted by the complaints of fee-paying residents.

William Townsend came into the house in 1716 with his wife and a maid. He was a man of means, paid slightly more for his accommodation than did the Monthly Meetings for the pauper residents, and valued himself extremely highly. He was to cause more trouble for Hutton than any other single individual. Because he thought himself better than the other residents he demanded special treatment. On one occasion the man who brewed the beer for the house asked Townsend 'why he found fault with the beer, it being very good. William told him, he loved to find fault when he saw faults for he had been cruelly used since he came here. The young man asked him wherein he had been so cruelly used, and if he had not his allowance? Aye, William said, but I pay more than the rest. The young man said, but if thou should have a different diet from the rest it would breed contention in the family. Then William said, but if they had been prudent managers they might have given us different from the rest and none of them have known it' (**84**). Hutton adamantly refused to give him better treatment, though he did what he could to keep the man quiet, and by doing so began a 'war' that stretched over a year and exercised Hutton's diplomatic skills to their limit. In this instance it was Hutton who strove to maintain equality within the house in the face of the objections of an inmate. He strove to ensure that all residents, including himself and his wife, had the same diet and treatment. William Townsend, and some others in a similar position, sought constant reinforcement for their own conceits, attempting to convert a largely egalitarian system to one which would have allowed them to play a dominant role in the management of the house (**80–88, 97**). Eventually, after many hard words and emotional scenes, which Hutton dutifully recorded, the workhouse committee forced Townsend out of the house, and gradually attempted to separate the children from the ancient friends.[52]

The Decline of the Co-operative Ideal

The house Hutton had entered in 1711 was losing money every year, failing to establish resources for its future security, and generally falling into disarray. When Hutton died in 1737, the house was regularly making a profit and had established its worth as a school. Moreover, it had amassed a large foundation which both cushioned it against temporary setbacks, and produced profits which could be used to subsidise the care of the inmates.

By 1737, it was also, however, far along the road from productive co-

---

52. See FSSWA, 'Best Minutes, 1714–1724', p. 179; Bolam, *Unbroken Community*, 51, 55.

operative to school, from John Bellers' idea of a self-supporting institution to an entirely paternalistic private school for the training up of Quaker children. The foundation which remained retained its kindness and humanity; there are letters from pauper children and inmates thanking Hutton and the committee for their extreme benevolence (**57, 58**), and likewise, there continued to be a strong emphasis on the co-operative aspect of the endeavour. Encouragement was continually given to the elderly to help one another and to form a 'workhouse family'. But once the elderly were relieved of the responsibility to work at their own trades, the labour done in the house became merely a means of encouraging a habit of industry among the young. The belief at the heart of Bellers' proposal, that the labour of the poor was the only 'standard to value all necessaries by . . .' and should be used for their benefit, became superfluous.[53]

This retreat from Bellers' pure statement of an humanitarian and co-operative tradition in poor relief was not acted out merely in the context of the Quaker workhouse. The broader tradition which had spawned the Corporations of the Poor was likewise first diluted and then subverted. It was not that the co-operative and humanitarian elements of the Corporations were ever completely eliminated, but that their repressive aspects loomed ever larger, while the faith in the value of the labour of the poor, upon which they were founded, was gradually undermined. In London the Corporation's first experiment in providing capital in the form of stock for the poor to work up was sabotaged by Sir Francis Child.[54] In Bristol, while an excellent example of the shrewdness and economic sophistication of the Corporation's founders can be seen in its first few years of operation, the Corporation was not allowed to remain successful for long. John Cary described the success of the Corporation in 1700: 'after about eight months time, our children could not get half so much as we expended in their provisions. The manufacturers who employed us, were always complaining . . . but would not advance above eight pence per pound for spinning . . . The committee voted that they would give employment to all the poor of the city . . . at the rates we offered to work, and pay them ready money for their labour. We soon found we had taken the right course, for in a few weeks we had sale for our fine yarn as fast as we could make it, and they gave us from eight pence, and were very well pleased with it.'[55] What the Corporation had done was to force up the price of pauper labour to something close to its real value by giving employment to all comers at a higher rate. The policy necessarily put other manufacturers at a disadvantage, and though extremely successful was not allowed to continue for long, spinning being replaced by the less remunerative and unskilled pauper manufacture of pin making,[56] an activity less central to the economy of Bristol and therefore less likely to affect the prosperity of the urban elite.

The Corporations struggled on in the 1700s and 1710s, the objects of

53. *First Worker Co-operators*, 13.
54. Macfarlane, 'Social Policy', 262.
55. Cary, *An Account of the Proceedings of the Corporation of Bristol*, 13–15.
56. Butcher, *Bristol Corporation of the Poor*, 7.

intense political strife in the cities they served,[57] but their role as manufacturing centres was steadily restricted and with that restriction went much of the justification for their existence. Even in their emasculated form the Corporations did retain elements of a co-operative and humanitarian tradition. There continued, in their management, to be an emphasis on the idea of a workhouse family, and they were still expected to provide the best possible care for the poor. But never, after their first few years, did they live up to the ideals inherent in the writings of their founders.

The Corporations had been an attempt to reflect the English tradition of poor relief in all its facets. They were superseded by a more successful attempt to subvert that tradition entirely. In the 1710s parochial workhouses began to be founded, small institutions serving small communities. The parochial workhouse movement was given support and central direction by the Society for Promoting Christian Knowledge and sought justification for its existence in an entirely different analysis of the social and economic role of workhouses. First, the SPCK and the founders of parochial houses were determined to use them as a means of strict control over the lives of the poor. Anyone sinful enough to end in a workhouse had first to be inured to labour, then brought to God, and through religion given a criterion for his behaviour, and finally through workhouse discipline forced to adopt an habitual and virtuous way of living.[58]

The second difference between the Corporation and parochial workhouses lay in the idea of a workhouse test. The Workhouse Test Act[59] was passed in 1722 as a result of the lobbying of the SPCK,[60] and in it was embodied the idea that a workhouse should form a deterrent, forcing the poor to seek any avenue for existence before resorting to the parish.

The later justifications for the existence of workhouses – that they should both mould the views and behaviour of inmates, and at the same time discourage the poor from exercising their right to poor relief – replaced the idea that, brought together in a co-operative environment, the poor could form a self-sufficient community. Indeed, in parochial workhouses, the labour of the poor was demanded not because it was profitable, but because it encouraged self-discipline. In an introduction to a SPCK pamphlet of 1725, the author asked, 'What great gains can be hoped for from old, infirm people who are past labour, or young unexperienced children who have everything to learn?', and answered his own question by suggesting that it would introduce 'among the poor, habits of sobriety, obedience and industry'.[61]

The parochial workhouse movement was largely successful. By 1777 over one per cent of the population was housed in deterrent work-

---

57. For examples see Macfarlane, 'Social Policy', 267–9; Hitchcock, 47, 49–52, 60–4, 83–5.
58. For a discussion of the role of the SPCK in the parochial workhouse movement see Hitchcock, 114–18, 224–34.
59. 9 Geo. I, c. 7.
60. Hitchcock, 127–8.
61. [Anon.], *An Account of Several Workhouses for Employing and Maintaining the Poor* (London, 1725), pp. iv, vi.

houses.[62] But the success of these institutions could not entirely destroy the humanitarian and co-operative traditions they sought to overlay. Even among the founders of these institutions there was an extreme reticence to put the idea of deterrence into practice. At Maidstone, for example, the parish could not bring itself to enforce a severe workhouse test and it continued to give weekly pensions after their house was opened though it was quite large enough to house all the parish poor, because, as Samuel Weller explained, 'we have many here who would choose to starve rather than be maintained in plenty and cleanliness in the Bridewell or house of correction as they call it.'[63] Similarly, there remained an expectation that somehow the inmates would form a workhouse family, that they would coalesce into a co-operative community.[64]

Moreover, among some writers on poor relief there remained the presumptions and aspirations of the writers and projectors of the 1690s and 1700s. In 1731 a series of broadsides was published by the Christian-Love Poor entitled *The Workhouse Cruelty; Workhouses turned Gaols and Gaolers turned Executioners*. Although these broadsides described specific scandals said to have taken place in the house belonging to St Giles in the Fields, their title indicates a belief that the function of workhouses had changed; that from being places of refuge for the poor, they had become places of confinement and punishment. Also, in the writings of Thomas Gilbert we can see all the aspects of the workhouse schemes of the 1690s. In these later writings there was still a degree of repression and paternalism, as there had been in the Corporations of the Poor, but likewise there was a belief that the poor should be brought together in a comfortable environment in which they could set about helping themselves.[65]

The mainstream of the English institutional poor-relief tradition was taken over by individuals advocating the use of workhouses as a deterrent, but there remained intact, as a subtext, a radical tradition of communal co-operativism, which was still there and ready to be drawn upon by nineteenth-century radicals and co-operators like Francis Place and Robert Owen.

The Quaker workhouse survived as well. In 1786, the institution moved to Croydon, Surrey, and the ancient friends were entirely separated from the children. Later, at the end of the nineteenth century, it moved again and became Friends' School at Saffron Walden, Essex, in which form it now survives.[66]

---

62. Over 90,000 people were housed in workhouses by 1777 according to a Parliamentary inquiry of that year. See HLRO, 'Poor Rate Returns, 1777', Parchment Collection, Box 162.
63. [Anon.], *Account of Several Workhouses* (1725), 35.
64. Ibid., pp. v–vi.
65. For example see Thomas Gilbert, *A Scheme for the Better Relief and Employment of the Poor; Humbly Submitted to the Consideration of His Majesty and the two Houses of Parliament* (London, 1764).
66. Bolam, *Unbroken Community*, 55, 116.

Note on Editorial Method

The original of 'Richard Hutton's Complaints Book' is currently (1986) held in the safe at Friends' School at Saffron Walden, the lineal descendant of the Quaker Workhouse at Clerkenwell, though as this volume goes to press arrangements are being made to have it and the school's other material transferred to the Essex Record Office, Chelmsford. It is a leather bound volume of 187 pages, written almost entirely in Hutton's own flowing hand. The volume is inaccurately paginated and shows the effects of Hutton's growing blindness; the handwriting grows larger towards the end of the 1720s and the number of entries per year declines significantly in the 1730s.

The manuscript is part of the school's very complete archive, which, for the first half of the eighteenth century, includes six volumes of workhouse committee minutes, rough drafts of the same minutes, a standing minute book with a separate index, eight volumes of general accounts, eleven volumes of ledgers, six bill books, a volume of material relating to legacies, and a complete admissions register. Some of the material contained in the complaints book, in particular the accounts and committee minutes, can also be found in other volumes in the archive.

For this edition, I have striven to eliminate as little relevant material as possible, and approximately nine-tenths of the book is reproduced here. There were in the original some items the inclusion of which would have served little purpose. The items excluded have been marked and briefly described in the text, and include first drafts of letters available in a more polished form elsewhere in the volume, and several pages of accounts. None of the accounts Hutton originally copied into the complaints book formed complete series, and as they are all available in the school's account and ledger books in a much more useful form it was not felt necessary to include more than a representative sample of them here. Bills of fare, house rules and questions asked of prospective inmates taken from the minute books are included as an appendix (**150–5**).

Spelling, punctuation and place names have been modernised, and personal names corrected to the individual's signature when available, and in accordance with the commonest available spelling where it is not. Sums of money have been translated into a standardised form. This edition is essentially a transcription, but occasionally additions and elisions of not more than one or two words have been made in order to clarify Hutton's prose. These have been indicated by the use of square brackets for additions and ellipses for elisions.

Most of the volume is written in Quaker 'plain language' and this usage has been retained. There is, however, one aspect of early eighteenth-century Quaker usage which it was felt necessary to modernise. Hutton normally wrote out his dates numerically as day, month, year, beginning his year from March, so that 7:12:1716 actually means 7 February 1717 in modern reckoning. In this edition Hutton's and all other dates in this form have been translated without comment into modern form.

Acknowledgements

I am grateful to the Governors of the Friends' School, Saffron Walden, for permission to publish this edition of Hutton's book.

The work of producing this volume has been greatly aided by a number of people. Chief among them is the archivist at Friends' School, Saffron Walden, Richard Wright. I would also like to thank the school's head, John C. Woods, and the staff at the Society of Friends' Library in London. I am also grateful for the comments and encouragement of Paul Slack, Penelope Corfield, Joanna Innes and John Styles. My original work on the Quaker Workhouse at Clerkenwell was made possible by the financial support of the Overseas Research Students Award Scheme. And finally, I would like to thank Sonia Constantinou, Nigel Quinney and Sheila Macdonald for their extreme tolerance. All of the mistakes in this volume are inevitably my own.

RICHARD HUTTON'S COMPLAINTS BOOK

1. [Inside front cover] 1717 Memorandum, March.
12 August, lent to Jonathan Burton, George Keith's *Way Cast Up.*[1]
16 August, and Bob Barclay's *Apology*[2] lent to W. Wall.
Stephen Crisp's *Works*[3] lent to Elizabeth Honnor.
Jacob Boehme's to Edward Durston.
Hospital at Hall in Germany[4] to Benjamin Mason.
Stephen Crisp's 3 volumes of sermons to Joseph Clutton, apprentice.
2 April, John Jeffreys, Webster's *On Bookkeeping.*[5]

> 1. George Keith, *The way cast up and the stumbling-blockes removed from before the feet of those who are seeking the way to Zion* (London, 1677).
> 2. Robert Barclay, *An apology for the true Christian divinity* (4th edn., London, 1678–9).
> 3. Stephen Crisp, *A memorable account of the Christian experiences* (London, 1694).
> 4. August Franck, *Piettas Hallensis: Or an abstract of the marvellous footsteps of divine providence in building a very large hospital . . . at Gloucha near Hall* (London, 1706).
> 5. William Webster, *An essay on book-keeping . . . by double entry . . . an attempt towards rendering the education of youth more easy and effectual* (London, 1721).

2. Loving friend John Heywood, I desire thee to take some care and notice of little Charles Toovey that is in the workhouse, that he may not do such work as spin mop yarn. I suppose thee knew his mother, Grace France that lived in London, an acquaintance of my husband's and mine, Joseph Chalk's wife's sister, of this town. I have a great respect for the child, he lived with me many years. I shall be glad to hear from thee and the child by the bearer. My dear love to the child. I rest with kind love to thyself from

thy loving friend,
P.P.
C.P.

Tuxbury 8 June 1719 &c.

3. [p. 1] From 29 September 1712 to 29 September 1716 the boys' earnings, including the profits of the yarn, comes to £567 2s. 6¾d.; the profit about £190 2s. 9d. . . .

4. [p. 2] Furmenty, milk pottage and pudding was made as followeth at the time we came into the house, viz:

To make furmenty formerly was put 12 quarts of milk, 12d. [worth of] wheat and 2½lb. of sugar.

Now, 15 quarts of milk, 12d. wheat and 2½lb. of sugar.

1

To make plum pudding was put 12 quarts of milk, 6lb. of suet, 4lb. of plums.

Now we put 15 quarts of milk, 10lb. of suet, 10lb. of plums. So for the advance of 3 quarts of milk we add 4lb. of suet & 6lb. of plums.

5. [An account of the finances of the house in 1716.]

6. [p. 3] Agreed with the baker that when the household bread is appointed in the weekly bill to weigh 16 ounces avoirdupois, that he shall take 8s. 6d. per hundredweight. And for every eight drams it alters in the weekly bill he will rise or fall 3d. per hundredweight in price as the following tables:

12 ounces avoirdupois	£ 10s. 6d.
12 ounces 8 drams	10s. 3d.
13 ounces	10s.
13 ounces 8 drams	9s. 9d.
14 ounces	9s. 6d.
14 ounces 8 drams	9s. 3d.
15 ounces	9s.
15 ounces 8 drams	8s. 9d.
16 ounces	8s. 6d.
16 ounces 8 drams	8s. 3d.
17 ounces	8s.
17 ounces 8 drams	7s. 9d.
18 ounces	7s. 6d.
18 ounces 8 drams	7s. 3d.
19 ounces	7s.
19 ounces 8 drams	6s. 9d.
20 ounces	6s. 6d.
20 ounces 8 drams	6s. 3d.
21 ounces	6s.
21 ounces 8 drams	5s. 9d.
22 ounces	5s. 6d.
22 ounces 8 drams	5s. 3d.
23 ounces	5s.
23 ounces 8 drams	4s. 9d.
24 ounces	4s. 6d.
24 ounces 8 drams	4s. 3d.
25 ounces	4s.
25 ounces 8 drams	3s. 9d.

7. [p. 4] To the committee, 11 May 1713.

Friends, some of the ancient friends being uneasy with the smallness of their allowance in diet, I thought it my place to let you know what they are now allowed, as also their allowance at the first settlement, by which you may see whether there is any just cause of complaint. The first bill of fare brought in may be seen at large . . . in the old minute book, page 28, **(151)** where they are allowed 7 oz. of butter and 14 oz. of cheese per week, and for every ounce more of butter to abate 2 oz. of cheese, 13 oz. of bread per day, 6 oz. of flesh per meal, 9 oz. of pudding per meal and furmenty &c a sufficient quantity.

And now by custom which continuance hath made a rule, they are allowed each: 8 oz. of butter and 16 oz. of cheese per week, about 14 oz. of bread (it not being weighed except Daniel Rosier's, who has 18 oz.) per day, 8 oz. of flesh per meal & if not enough they are desired to send for more, 19 oz. of pudding per meal, and more if they can eat it (which is 10 oz. per meal more than the former allowance), furmenty, milk &c a sufficient quantity, to some a quart. So friends be pleased to take in consideration some methods you think fit or a new bill of fare, the diet in some respects being altered, that there may be no uneasiness in the family or reflecting on the plentiful provisions of the house, either at home or abroad; which has very lately been done, besides the . . . hard censures I and my wife are under having the management under you.
Workhouse   Richard Hutton

8. [p. 5] Some of John Gorden's behaviour in the house.
Besides several faults too tedious to mention here, he lately pick[ed] one boy's pocket of six pence and another of three pence and ran away and spent it. And at another time he went to a neighbour's and told them he had not victuals enough and desired trust for buns &c. He had then stole a knife and fork from [a] boy and one of the house knives and sold them for three half pence, which, when I knew, I sent for again, since we found a knife in his pocket belonging to the house. At another time he got a candle over night and got up about twelve a clock at night and took a pane of glass out of the storeroom window and got in, from whence he took about four pounds of plum pudding, although he, as well as the rest of the big boys, had a full pound for dinner besides their suppers. And he ate so much in the storeroom he could not come thence without leaving behind him what is not fit here to mention. And about a week ago he privately stole the key of the street door. Towards night we suspected him and tasked him with it, but he confidently denied with such a countenance, as if he had really been innocent, so that we searched diligently for it a great while, but in vain which made us very uneasy. However, about 5 next morning we went up where he lay and asked him about it again, but he denied it. Then we made him come out of bed and found the key under him. He intended, as he confessed, to have taken the knives out of the drawers and to have sold them with the key. We have since kept him as close as we can but he has been up, dressed in the middle of the night for what intent we do not certainly know, for there is no believing him; so that every day we are in danger of having things stole, and every night of some misfortune or other [p. 6] for he said openly to the ostler, if any body should fire . . . the hay in the stable he believed it would burn the house or something to that purpose. And nobody knows but he may at one time or another put such bad thoughts in practice. And if at any time he is corrected for his faults, he cuts his truss and lets down his rupture, so that we find him not only to be a very bad example to the rest of the children, but indeed very unsafe to live in such a house as this is.

9. [A list of bills due to the workhouse, 7 December 1713.]

10. In order to settle the accounts in the ledger and then find the stock or state of the house, as also the gain or loss in any one desired time:

1st Post the cash and expense book &c into the ledger to the day intended to balance, and the linen book.

2d Procure the bills of all such debts as are owing to workmen for repairs, the farrier for shoeing, for grazing, provisions, coals, wool &c or whatsoever money is due from the house.

Also the total of all the debts due to the house whether for yarn, spinning, mops &c or anything else.

3d Beginning at the first page in the ledger and proceeding to the last page: charge. Charge each monthly meeting (in this house as pensioners) with their quarterly allowances for their board and each tenant with their quarterly payment of rent and give each servant credit on their account for their quarterly wages.

4th Weigh all the yarn in the house, as also take an account of the mops remaining unsold and find the weight of the wool unspun thus:

Add one part in four, but clean middle wool or good locks one part in five, of the weight of all the yarn that is made of the wool that is spinning at the time of balancing to the whole weight of the said yarn, and subtract the sum from the weight of the wool first bought. The remainder is the weight of the wool (as near as can be supposed) remaining in the house unspun. Used mops to wear and tear.

[p. 7] 5th See what provision, malt &c, rests in the house.

6th Find what taxes is due on the house and tenements at the time of balancing.

7. Write out the horse bill for the meeting of twelve and all other horse bills if any.

8. See what hay, corn, straw &c remains unspent and take the same of the coals burnt since the last balancing from the coals then remaining in the house. The remainder is the present stock in coals.

9. Write out the monthly meetings' bills and all bills due to the house of whatsoever sort.

10. Subtract the wear and tear of the brewing vessels to the time we balance to, from the sum that hath been laid out on them to the said time whether for prime cost, repair cost or improvements. The remainder is the stock in brewing vessels.

And to find the loss by the wear of them in the time between the balancing, take what sum is laid out on them in the said time from the wear and tear of them in the same and the remainder is what's required.

11. Settle every account in the ledger and find both the stock and loss or gain thereon, thus:

Add up the debtor side, then the creditor side. Charge whatsoever sum is owing for that account (as particularly as bills due to workmen &c in repairs, all money due for taxes in the account of taxes, all bills due to the farrier, grass, hay, corn &c as also the ostler's board and wages in the stable account [)]. Add the said debts to the sum of the debtor side and proceed to add up the creditor side of the same account, and under the sum charge all debts due to that account (as horse bills &c in the stable account), as also whatever remains in the house (as yarn, wool and mops in the wool account . . . and as hay and corn in the stable accounts . . . and provision in the house expenses). Add the said stock to the sum of the creditor side and compare the debtor side therewith by subtracting one from the other. And if the debtor side appear to be more than the creditor side the difference is the loss on that account, there having been more laid out thereon than the income & stock will defray, but if the creditor side exceed the debtor there is so much gained as the one is more than the other.

[p. 8] To make the account balance add the difference under the title of profit and loss to that side as is wanting. So shall the account be finished as was required.

And whatsoever sum or sums is charged as stock on the creditor side of any account in order to the balancing, it must be transferred to the debtor side of that account for the next quarter's stock, which sum or sums will be the stock of the same account in the state of the house.

And whatsoever sum or sums is charged on the debtor side of any account in order to balancing it must come on the creditor side of the same account for the next quarter and will be what the stock or state of the house must make good or pay and therefore be debtor. For excepting the ostler's board and wages, which must be dropped as stock, he being servant to the stable and receiving his wages from them, the stable should be debtor to his service. Yet his service being employed in the said account already balanced cannot be a stock for the time to come.

12. Upon a piece of waste paper or rather in the bill book, collect what's due to all servants for wages to the time of balancing.

13. Also collect (in the said book) the rent due from each tenant into one sum till the time of balancing.

14. To find the stock or state of the house:

Having things in such a readiness as is above directed, on a sheet of paper write, stock debtor per contra creditor with the day of the month. First, to give stock credit by the total of each bill due from the monthly meetings and all other bills due from any persons for allowances with collecting them by any method out of the ledger. Because . . . they stand scattered throughout the said ledger, for which its advised to enter the bills first. Then beginning at the letter A in the alphabet in the ledger, proceed alphabetically to the letter Z and in whatsoever account there appears anything remaining in or due to the house let the same be carried to the creditor side of the stock.

And on the contrary, in whatsoever account there appears to be anything due from the house, or that the house oweth . . . let the same be carried to the debtor side of the stock.

Subtract the debtor side from the creditor; the remainder is the neat or clear stock or state of the house.

[p. 9] 15. To find the profit and loss balance:

In the bill book collect the bare allowance (without anything paid for necessaries) of each monthly meeting out of the bills and carry the sums of each to the creditor side of the balance. Note: if the balance is for one

5

quarter, collect the bills for one quarter, but if the balance be for a longer time collect the allowance for the same time. And always remember to collect the allowances from the commencement of the balance to its ending. Observe this method through all the accounts in balancing.

The reason whereof is because the income of any quarter &c is only proper to compare with the expenses of the same quarter &c. In order to find the gain or loss therein:

Collect all the rents contracted by the tenants between the balance into one sum and carry the same to the debtor side of the balance.

Beginning at A in the alphabet in the ledger and proceeding to the Z, in whatsoever account there appears to be any gains let the same (whether for $\frac{1}{4}$ year, $\frac{1}{2}$ year &c, or for what time we purpose to balance) be carried to the creditor side of the balance.

And by whatsoever account there appears to be any loss, let the same loss be carried to the debtor side of the balance.

Compare the sum of the debtor side of the balance with the sum of the creditor side and find the total gain or loss.

So is the balance ended or finished.

11. [p. 10] As there is nothing does more universally commend a man to any office or employment as to be a dextrous and ready penman and accurate accomptant, so there is nothing can be more pleasing to the ingenious or universally acceptable to mankind than to trace and chalk out such a method as will infallibly help and assist them in attaining those qualifications which are so useful and necessary, so much wished for and desired by all ranks and degrees of men. Some few years after I had first begun to teach school I observed frequent complaints of youth not being able readily to apply to business what they learned at the writing school, notwithstanding they were capable to write a pleasant fair hand in a copy book after the master's copy. Now the main ground and reason of this complaint I conceive chiefly to be, first of all because many youths . . . have not sufficient time allowed them to acquire a natural freedom of habit or writing before they go forth to prentice. Although they may have learned a fair character, they learned at their writing school. Secondly, the natural tendency of youth to sloth and idleness, a neglect of their practise and a want of keeping up to the character they learned at writing school. Thirdly, their not being employed at school to write other business besides their copies. Now as the two first causes do many time arise from themselves and those that dispose of them, so the latter may some times proceed from their master or teacher. This put me on a design of curing as well as I could this general complaint by employing some scholars at night and other times to write without lines either the forms of letters, acquittances, receipts or six or eight verses out of the Bible, or some other book. Some times I made them write out my tradesman's copy book, the forms of bills of sale, the methods of keeping a cash book &c. Sometimes they copied out their sums and rules of arithmetic, which method I found so successful that many scholars could write . . . without a copy as well as with one; which experience drew from me the method here presented you in this book, which has not failed of its desired success where duly applied. I found it very helpful to such dull youths as had spent a great deal of their time at the Latin school to so little purpose that they know not how to write or spell English in any tolerable measure. It was also of great use to the children of the poor ordinary tradesmen, whose parents' [p. 11] poverty cannot spare so much money nor yet allow their children to spend so many years at the grammar school as is necessary to qualify them in that desired accomplishment of writing true English. I find the poorer sort of people (I cannot learn how thus unhappily misled) think if they can but send their children to the Latin school for two or three years it will be a means to make them understand and write true English; whereas it will require much more time than they can commonly well allow them at the grammar school before their child can be thoroughly capable to apply his grammatical learning in order to make him such a writer of English as they intend.

By what is here offered in relation to the children of poor people, and such whose capacities can never attain the Latin tongue, I would not be presented as an enemy to Latin, which is a noble, useful and excellent accomplishment. But it requires the assistance of an able purse, good parts and sufficient time to go through the classical authors to be rendered true grammarians. Now should none learn the Latin tongue but such as had parts fit for it, and had the other qualities before mentioned to make it truelly useful to them, our public schools would be found almost sufficient to teach such youths the Latin and other . . . learned tongues, and the greatest number of private school masters might find themselves employment enough to teach the rest of our youths the true use and knowledge of their own mother tongue. For . . . [then] the poor handicraft tradesman [could] be persuaded to keep their children wholly to the English school till they could read pronounce and spell any word distinctly, and understand the meaning of what they read (which will be difficult to do without the use [of] English dictionaries) were this method well observed. And that those I warn of private grammar schools (especially in the out parts of the town[)], all of them pretending to teach Latin, Greek and Hebrew, if the most of these learned gentlemen could be prevailed with to teach nothing but English, and would take care to learn their scholars to make good English exercise, which is altogether as useful and necessary, and almost as difficult, as to make good Latin, the poor would find it much more for their children's profit and advantage than to murder three or four years time in the learning Latin to little or no [p. 12] purpose.

And herein I appeal to thousands that miserably suffer by their education for want of true knowledge of the English tongue. If the parents design their children for the mechanic or handicraft they should send them to the drawing schools (to spend some part of the day there for three or four years) rather than to the Latin school; by which means the kingdom would in a few years be furnished with the best artists and workmen in the world.

The poor are generally very solicitous to give their children learning and spare for no cost in their power to make them happy in that respect; it being a common saying with them that learning is all the portion they can give them, and a very good one too, if well directed. Which consideration has, in great measure, drawn from me so large a preface.

We are very apt to cry up the French and other foreigners for writers; and to do them justice many of them write well, natural and free; and so may most in England too, if they'd pursue the same method, viz: by an early considering which way to dispose of their children in the world. I have been informed that if they design them for trade or clerkship in France, Holland and other countries beyond sea, they rarely discontinue them from the writing schools. Now after a youth comes once to a natural habit of writing well, two or three hours in a week with a writing master will both keep it up and improve it. For it is rare to find any so excellent as those whose art grows up with their years by which it becomes natural habit with them.

That so many amongst us can never be brought to write so dextrously well, notwithstanding the art of writing was never at more perfection than now, is because . . . as soon as children can make their letters and put them together that their Latin master can just read their exercise, they are commonly taken off from the writing school before any habit is acquired, and then six or seven years or more is spent in a continual scribble of their exercise. And the usual saying is, a quarter or two at the writing master's just before they go apprentice will do the work, not considering that it is a task much more difficult for any master to teach and break the ill habits, than it is at first to teach. And then that which they formerly most slighted is now most coveted and desired as being like to be of greatest use and service to them in the whole course of their life. But by reason of ill contracted habits [p. 13] cannot be so easily (if ever) attained to that perfection which is desired. It is not to be denied but any that is a master of writing, and understands to demonstrate the reason of letters, may teach a lad of a competent genius, that never learned before, to write a fair legible hand in a month or six weeks' time or less. But yet it requires some considerable time to make that writing habitual, natural and free to them; and indeed it is for want of that, and of constant practice, as we said before, and care of keeping to the character after youths are taught, that there are such frequent complaints they can do so little when they come into the shop or counting house. Now to enable youths to write as readily in the shop book as their copy book and to prepare them for business, I could think of nothing proper for their excercise and practice at night when they left school than the alphabet of names to make them ready in great letters and spell any names, the contraction of words to dispatch business, bills of parcel accompts taken out of the debt book, bills of exchange, both foreign and domestic &c [and] forms of country chapman's letters . . . The frequent writing out of these and such like sometimes for tasks, I found to be an excellent means to enable youths to perform their business, and write things readily and freely of hand.

For after a youth has formed his hand at the writing school, if he would write neat and free in a short time, he must write much and elsewhere besides his copy book. And parents . . . [should] think their children . . . [a] part of their care . . . [and] look better after them than many do, and find them some business to employ them either in writing bills or copy letters after they come home from school, and not suffer them to play about streets and leave all to the child's master as if they had no interest or concern in the matter.

In the whole, I have endeavoured to make the book as universally practical as is possible in so short a compass; and though some things relating to merchandise may be above the capacity of such teachers as are ignorant of accompts, yet the greatest part of it is proper for the most common and ordinary trades, and of great use to such as teach scholars writing, arithmetic and accompts. Having had experience how defective the most ingenious youths (many times) are in practical parts of business, I have here given them the forms of several foreign invoices and accounts of sales to instruct them as well in method as in casting up [p. 14] and reducing the foreign coin to Sterling money. Lastly, as an appendix, I have framed such questions in numeration, addition, subtraction, multiplication and division &c to the rule of three, that will very much assist youths in the right understanding the rules aforesaid, which too many are ignorant of even after they have run through all the rules in arithmetic. That youth may not only have the forms of business in trade, but also a fair copy to imitate after they go apprentice, I have engraved a book called the *Apprentices Companion, or, Tradesman's Copy Book*, wherein receipts, bills of parcels, bills of debts, bills of exchange, accounts of sales, and the form of a cash book &c are all fairly written in the merchant-like running hand now in use, designed for an assistance to this book. Now if this book be carefully written and gone over two or three times at the writing school it must necessarily set a lad a year forward or more in the service of his master, by which it will be a great pleasure to his master to have a servant so capable of his service. And again, it will make the apprentice's business more delightful and pleasant and his service more easy when he readily understands how to perform his business and please his master. To render this book further useful with the large addition now added, I will conclude with some short observations concerning the regular making and orderly ranking of figures, which to perform nicely is esteemed a qualification almost equal to that of a good hand. And since none of the ancient or modern school masters (that I know of) have yet undertaken to instruct us in the English, French and Italian method of ranking figures, I have adventured to offer some thoughts about it. I observe there is now in use, two ways or orders of ranking figures . . . One is the old way (heretofore generally used) following the order of the Roman print, in which the figures are mostly set upright as 1, 2, 3, 4, 5, 6, 7, 8, 9, 10, where you may observe that only 1, 2, 0, stands upon the line, except 6 and 8 whose heads are as much above the top of 1, 2, 0, as the tails of 3, 4, 5, 7 & 9 are made to come below the line. From whence may be derived this general rule viz: those figures which are not lineal, i.e., of an equal height and depth in the order of the nine figures, may yet by accident become lineal when they happen in conjunction together, as 3, 4, 5, 7, 9, and 8 & 6. The 6 in my opinion will not properly become lineal with any of the figures except the 8, only as 86.

12. [p. 15: Blank in the original]

13. [p. 16] About Hannah Doggett's legacy, 28 February 1716.
To the friends of Hammersmith Monthly Meeting,

Whereas there was a matter in difference long depending between Richard Kirton and Richard Hawkins, executors of Hannah Doggett, and a member of your monthly meeting on two accounts in the first place, for a just debt conceived by unjustly keeping us out of the possession of a tenement which that member of yours lives in. Upon which unwarrantable procedure we, in a gospel manner, dealt with the said person and waited for some fruit from her who you were in unity with. But this our labour proving fruitless, we, the executors, thereupon complained of your abuse to your meeting, and as the party was your member we desired the meeting would do us justice by making use of their power to oblige such, their member, to do what was just. For in case they by their authority should not prevail according to equity, truth and a good conscience, . . . then we the executors might be at liberty to take our remedy as the law directs. Upon . . . your meeting we waited a considerable time, but met with no redress and did therefore again make our appeal both in word and writing. Yet, notwithstanding all our endeavours the party was supported as a friend in truth and we by that means prevented of the justice. All which we look upon to proceed either by the neglect of the meeting or by the encouragement given by some of such as were prevailing members thereof, by which means for six years we were made by the said party, thus screened, matter of derision and scorn. And in that exalted state made her will and therein carried on the fraud so far as to bequeath the said tenement and terms of years unexpired to her executors. All which according to our understanding, had the meeting discharged themselves in justice, might have been prevented and as thus otherwise managed. We desire now to know of the meeting whether [p. 17] according to this their management they have not drawn upon themselves to be answerable to us, the executors, for the money as of right we ought to have had of the person by them under the profession of truth all along thus protected. So desiring your consideration herein and your answer thereto, we remain your friends in the truth.

Richard Kirton
Richard Hawkins

14. An answer to the foregoing letter.
Friends Richard Kirton and Richard Hawkins,
Yours dated 28 February 1716 was received and well read in our meeting to which it was directed and as you desired. [It was] considered and we were surprised and troubled that you should render our meeting not only supporters of one of our members in refusing a just debt, but with neglect and also with being preventers of justice and that we or some prevailing members of our meeting screened their member and thereby caused you to be derided and scorned in that they did [not] prevent the injustice you complain of.

To which we answer, having perused our minutes, we do not find or are we conscious that we have so done or are anyways guilty of supporting any in refusing any just debt or with neglect of justice and [having] caused you to be derided and scorned . . . Therefore we look upon your charges [as] harsh and undue & hope upon better considerations you will retract them. As to what you propose to our meeting's consideration, (viz) whether our management has not brought upon ourselves to be answerable to you for what the deceased . . . [p. 18] member owed, being as you say all along protected. Answer: we suppose you mean A. Aldworth and upon consideration we find no reason for your charge on us nor cause we have to pay her debts, for [we] are not her executors. Besides, you tell us not the sum, nor for whose use we should pay it to you who are executors for Hannah Doggett in trust for us and the two other meetings to pay the improvements of Little Holland House, ground and appurtenances, not a part only but of the whole; and in our judgement if any less be we lose, for we are not willing you should be at any loss for repairs . . . Why then can not you and we be easy, for we hope and have that charity to believe you do not intend to take any of the profits into your own pockets. Be pleased therefore to give an account how much improvements hath been made of the lease and what loss (if any hath been) and what allowed for taxes and other charges that you have been at, that persuant to the donors instructions, her will may be answered and . . . we may have our share of the profits of the lease (and not a part only). The meeting having rejected Richard Hawkins' proposals after it was referred to the three meetings to determine; . . . those, the several meetings chosen, are of opinion the whole improvements belong to them.

So with our loves we remain your friends hoping you'll readily comply to answer the will of the donor as the three meetings have unanimously agreed.

From our monthly meeting at Hammersmith held by adjournment the 22 March 1716.

Signed in behalf of the said meeting by
Thomas Crow

15. [p. 19] The state of the case relating to Hannah Doggett's legacy. Hannah Doggett survives her husband and by will gives unto Richard Hawkins and Richard Kirton the lease of Little Holland House, which her husband and Richard Aldworth . . . [had] of the Lady Holland [and] which was to go to the survivors. See the lease.

Hannah Doggett in her private instructions bearing equal date with her will declares it is her mind and will that the said Richard Hawkins and Richard Kirton should pay the improvements of the lease unto the Savoy [and] Hammersmith Monthly Meetings and the workhouse in equal proportion, for the relief or benefit of the poor under the care of the said meetings; and something hath by them been paid accordingly.

But about [blank in the original] Richard Hawkins came to the Savoy or Hammersmith Monthly Meeting or both, informs that the executors had been at charge to repair, and proposed if they would pay for the repairs they then, i.e. Richard Hawkins and Richard Kirton, would pay unto the said three meetings as their gift, not as their right, £5 per anno [in] equal proportion for the remaining part of the lease, which if the meetings would not accept they may expect nothing.

Which Hammersmith Meeting were not willing to accept because they esteemed it was their right by the donor's will to have their share of the improvements.

And Hammersmith nominated three friends, and the other two meetings nominated each three friends, and they [were] to enquire and give their judgements which they did and unanimously agreed and gave it under their hands that the right of the lease or improvements thereof according to the donor's mind belongs to friends.

[p. 20] But Richard Hawkins and Richard Kirton were otherwise minded and alleged it was only the part which Hannah Doggett lived in that the meeting had a right unto; which if so (notwithstanding the money which had been laid out by Hannah Doggett[)] that part . . . fell short of producing with that improvement, £20 per annum and then there would be nothing for the poor of the three meetings.

So the friends appointed by the three meetings then desired to see Hannah Doggett's private instructions, but Richard Hawkins said they were lost.

But by friends' records of wills, truths and instructions of donors they found they were entered. Richard Hawkins according to friends' method & order carried them in.

And by the private instructions they found that it was . . . the improvements of the whole taken of the Lady Warwick which the three meetings had a right unto.

Then the Hammersmith Meeting desired to have an account what the improvements hath been since Hannah Doggett's death and what hath been paid thereof and what charges the executors had been at, for as their names were only made use of in this gift to convey it to the poor of the said three monthly meetings they did not judge it reasonable they should sustain any loss thereby and hope they do not intend to make any gain thereby or profit to themselves, conceiving it never was the intent of the donor.

But such an accompt Hammersmith Meeting had not yet obtained. A letter indeed was sent to the said meeting wherein the meeting accounts they are unduely (to say no more) charged. And as answer was earnestly pressed for, the meeting sent one and desired again an accompt what improvements had been made, what paid, also what charges the executors had been at for repairs. But they, Richard Hawkins and Richard Kirton, say it's no answer, so they give not any account, which Hammersmith . . . [p. 21] Meeting do not esteem so fair and friendly as they might expect, considering that for the whole lease there is but £20 paid per annum, and towards that, John Castard [pays] £15 for a part which Hannah Doggett lived in, . . . and £2 more for a little house, and £6 for that part of the ground A. Aldworth had. So they receive £23 and pay £[blank] . . . besides considerable they understand hath been received for that house which is part of the lease given, as aforesaid, which Alice Aldworth lived in.

If the improvements will not pay for the repairs when the executors give an account as desired, . . . ways and means should be thought on by the three meetings as apprehended to reimburse them.

But if the executors and the nine friends from the aforesaid meetings cannot adjust to satisfaction then it may be (it is conceived) referred to some others that may be chosen or to the six weeks meeting in London [**25, 27**].

16. [p. 22] Counsel's advice concerning the oath commonly taken by those that are elected constables.
Being informed that Richard Basnett at the last court leet holden for the manor within which the Liberty of Norton Full Gate lieth, was duly elected one of the head boroughs for the said liberty and that thereupon the steward of the said county required him to take the said office upon him and told him that he would not require an oath of him for the execution thereof in respect of his opinion; . . . the question being whether the said Richard Basnett may lawfully & safely execute the said office without taking the said oath:

I conceive clearly that he may, because it is the election which makes him an officer & not the oath, which is but a mere strict obligation upon him for the due execution of his office. There is no law or statute to make his acting void or penal to him for want of taking the oath. And the steward of the leet (who was the proper person to swear him) having dispensed with giving the oath, I conceive it is . . . not the concern of any justice of the peace to enquire whether he was sworn or not. And I do not find any law or statute to impower any justice of the peace to swear constables, but only to swear under-sheriffs and their bailiffs, who have return of writs from courts of records, as the statute of the 27th of Queen Elizabeth and the 12th chapter and of the 11th of Henry the 7th & the 15 chapter.

Thomas Corbet
London, 14 November 1677.

17. The Cambridgeshire case on the other side.
[p. 23] This is to inform such friends of truth as are concerned or prosecuted upon the statute made against popish recusants in the 23d & 29th year of Queen Elizabeth, and the 3d year of King James, which ordains and inflicts upon every person not conforming himself unto the liturgy of the Church of England the penalty of twenty pounds per month for not repairing to the parish church to hear divine service (so called):

That thirteen friends in Cambridgeshire who were lately prosecuted and convicted as offenders against the said statute, had their goods levied and two thirds of their estates seized upon that account into the King's hands, did all appear in Cambridge the last Lent assizes held for that county, the 8th day of the month called March 1680, before the Lord Chief Baron [William] Montague, then judge of assize for the same county. And thereupon said thirteen friends, all . . . of them severally, took the test before him which test is a solemn declaration as hereafter is expressed (above the form of the judges' certificate) according to the Act of Parliament made in the thirtieth year of King Charles the Second (entitled an act for the more effectual preserving of his majesties person and government[)].[1] Of which the Chief Baron did certify and acquaint the King in Easter term last, whereupon the King did signify it was his pleasure that all the said friends should be discharged upon the account of the prosecution. Whereof the King's Attorney General did inform all the Barons of the Exchequer in open court and thereupon the courts did immediately order that all further process against the friends should be stayed for the future . . . General seizures and . . . levies should be likewise foreborn upon the aforesaid penalties of 20 pounds a month [p. 24] and accordingly the said order was drawn up and passed throughout all offices in Trinity term last: 1681 for the discharge of all those friends in general. And they are now discharged accordingly whose names are as followeth, viz: Francis Emerson, Richard Webb, Thomas Amey, Richard Pellett, Edward Cooke, Edward Smith, John Prime, Henery Bostock, John Harvey, Robert Salmon, Jacob Baker, John Salmon, Ann Dockura.

1. See 30 Chas. II, stat. 2.

18. [The Test: see 30 Chas II, stat. 2]

19. [p. 25] Judge's certificate.
These are humbly to certify the King's most excellent majesty that the persons . . . above written came before me this [blank] day of [blank] anno: dom. 1681 at [blank] & did severally voluntarily make and subscribe the declaration contained in an Act of Parliament made Anno Tricesimo Carolium Regis &c: and entitled, 'An act for the more effectual preserving his majestys person and government by disabling Papists from sitting in either House of Parliament', witness my hand this [blank] day of [blank] 1681.

20. At Appleby Assizes, 1681, those judges, viz: Judge Dolben and Judge Gregory, were very moderate towards friends and moved the justices of the peace to see friends subscribe the test in order to their release from the statutes of Queen Elizabeth and King James for £20 per mensem on the account of recusancy or being prosecuted among Papists . . . They (to wit) Justice Fleming and others very readily accepted . . . and hereby many friends are let at liberty both as to person & estate who took the said test which also clears them of being counted Papists . . .

21. [p. 26] Thomas Taylor's solemn declaration to clear himself from that wicked aspersion of being a Jesuit and from Popery &c.
I, Thomas Taylor, do in the presence of almighty God solemnly profess and in good conscience declare it is my real judgement that the Church of Rome is not the church of Christ nor the Pope or Bishop of Rome Christ's vicar and that his or her doctrine of deposing heretical princes and absolving their subjects of their obedience, of purgatory and prayers for the dead, of indulgences and worshipping of images, of adoring and praying to the Virgin Mary and other saints deceased and of transubstantiation or changing the elements of bread and wine into the body & blood of Christ at or after the consecration thereof by any person whatsoever are false erroneous and contrary to the truth of God declared in the Holy Scriptures and therefore the communion of the said church is superstitious and idolatrous.

And I do likewise sincerely testify and declare that I do, from the bottom of my heart, detest and abhor all plots and conspiracies that are or may be contrived against the King, Parliament or people of this realm. And I do hereby promise, with God's help, to live a sober and peaceable life as becometh a good Christian and Protestant to do. And all this I do acknowledge, intend, declare and subscribe without any equivocation, or mental reservation, according to the true plainness, simplicity and usual significance of the words.

Stafford,
7 June 1679.

Witness my hand,
Thomas Taylor

22. [p. 27] Dear George Whitehead,
Thy labour of love in this present business of mine and the truth's is kindly received, and thy reward rests with thee in thy own bosom, where our heavenly father abundantly answers and satisfies his children in and for their services for his name's sake. So be it.

I have here enclosed, sent, subscribed, my testimony (as friends have given) against Popery. To show as need is in the Lord's power and patience I shall overcome all. For so from the beginning has been victory, having done . . ., in the light, what the Lord hath given us to see to be our duty. To leave all to him whom but the winds and seas obey. In whose dear peace in tender love to thee, thy wife and all friends, with prayers to the Lord for his presence and assistance, with you in all your holy affairs at this and all times, with his protection over you, rests,

Thine dearly in Christ Jesus,
Stafford, 7 June 1679   Thomas Taylor

23. [p. 28] Directions for the school mistress to observe.
Having had under our consideration the management of the girls we think it convenient:

In summer, from the time the sun riseth at six, and sets at six, they should write in the mornings till breakfast time, and after breakfast to go to sewing work &c till dinner, & after dinner till the evening.

And in the winter to sew one morning & write &c another . . . and in afternoons go to sewing.

And that two or three or more of the biggest and most handy of the girls be ready as occasion requires to assist in the family especially at washing times, and the school mistress to instruct them in getting up her and their linen and that the same girls have opportunity to be helpful in the kitchen and elsewhere.

And that she take care to instruct the girls and see that their linen, stockings &c be kept timely in repair and their shoes tight and all their clothes in decent order and when put off carefully put in a proper place.

And that she attend them at meal times to see them of a good behaviour and as often as may be to have an eye over them when from school.

And that she be willing to be directed in her management if occasion requires, and entirely refrain any secret correspondence with the children's parents, or the ancient friends, or servants of the family and

15

discourage whispering in all against the government of the house.
5 June 1716.

24. [p. 29] Please to consider if it were not convenient before the school mistress be agreed with she first appear at the women's meeting to be recommended by them as one fit to teach the children of this house, which we are of opinion the women friends do expect and believe it may be satisfaction to the children's parents and others to have a woman the said meeting esteem a proper person and qualified.

The necessary expense of this house is about £3 per week . . . And we may reasonably conclude when we have a school mistress the number of girls will much increase, which if they do to 30 at 12d. per week the house will lose by them only (especially if the mistress have their work) about £156 per year.

And though we do not say the girls earn 12d. per week by their spinning, yet we have found by the quick return and good price . . . the yarn hath borne, the profit arising from the trade of the yarn made by them amounts to more than 12d. per week each.

So that if the school mistress have the profit of the work we compute the loss to the house will be about £100 per year more than now it is for the maintenance of about 30 girls and more or less as there is a greater or a lesser number.

And if the house has the profit of the children's sewing work &c it may be questioned whether it will pay a mistress's board and wages, buy thread, needles, samplers, silk-worsted &c for some considerable time while the children are all of them unlearnt.

We propose no profit by letting the school mistress have the children's work, yet we have hope if the house is encouraged by sending in linen &c, in time the children may be brought to something to some profit. And it is our opinion it would be more reputable and may prove more profitable to give the school mistress a salary, also thereby the improvement of the children may be more easily seen, their earnings necessarily coming into the accounts.

[p. 30] Note: the design of making these observations is not in the least to hinder the having of a school mistress for the girls, because we daily experience the absolute necessity thereof both for the advantage of the girls in their education and for the reputation of the house, but the design is to show the necessity of procuring such an one who shall sincerely use all endeavours to make the business as much to the profit of the house as possibly she can.

25. Richard Hawkins and Richard Kirton's letter to the committee 22 June 1716 [see **13–15, 27**].
Friends,

We received by your order a minute dated 4 June the which comparing with that received in August last hath caused some considerations in us how such an alteration of temper should have gotten place. Yet notwithstanding the threats of some and harsh speeches of others, who may take upon them to be judges in their own cause, we shall still endeavour to answer a good conscience in justice both to . . . them we are concerned for, as also in some measure what relates to ourselves, for had we been in that warmth as we seem now to be treated with, we query whether for so many years past some, were they under our circumstances, would not have insisted on having security to indemnify them for the £20 per annum we lie liable under to pay for the ground rent. The which, having born with silence hitherto, do now insist upon. The which when done we shall be far from giving you cause of complaint or troubling of the six weeks meeting as that, on the contrary, we shall be willing to refer the matter when remaining to some friends that may be indifferently chosen, and in the mean time rests your friends and brethren.

Richard Kirton
Richard Hawkins

26. [p. 31] East India stock.
Whereas by transfer bearing even date with these present and entered in the transfer book of the United East India Company, Thomas Martin of London, goldsmith, did assign and transfer five hundred pounds East India stock or credit unto Benjamin Mason, George Wingfield & Edward Burford. Now we, the said Benjamin Mason, George Wingfield and Edward Burford, do hereby for us respectively and for our respective executors and administrators declare and agree that the said five hundred pounds stock so transferred unto us aforesaid and the dividends to accrue thereon shall be vested in and enjoyed by us equally, share and share alike during our joint lives, but that upon the death of any of us the said stock and the dividends to be then after made thereon shall go unto and be enjoyed by the two survivors during their joint lives, and that upon the death of either of the said two survivors, the said stock and all the dividends & profits to be from that time made thereon shall go unto and be enjoyed by the longest liver of us, and the executors and administrators of such longest liver, to his and their proper use & behoof forever. In witness whereof we the said Benjamin Mason, George Wingfield and Edward Burford have hereunto set our respective hands and seals this 22d day of February 1717.

27. [p. 32] Hannah Doggett's private instructions [**13–15, 25**].
The lease of Little Holland House to be disposed of and the profit equally divided between the three several [monthly] meetings hereafter named: Hammersmith, Savoy and Friends' Workhouse.

   And the nine pounds given by me to be dispursed amongst twelve poor friends of the Bull Quarter: ten shillings a piece. And the like to six in the Savoy Quarter. Her clause without a date.

28. [p. 33] Dispursements of Thomas Coxe's legacy.
4 March 1712

To make lining, buttons and pockets per a pair of breeches for Mo Lee	2s. 9d.
To ditto Edward Bates	2s. 9d.
To ditto Samuel Cooper	2s. 9d.

To making breeches & waistcoat &c per Joseph Hilton	5s.
To make breeches &c Tho. Taylor	2s. 9d.
To ditto for Prince Scott	2s. 9d.
To ditto per John Hall	2s. 9d.
	————
	£1. 1s. 6d.

29. 3 April 1712

To 44 yards of plain cloth at 2s. 6d. per yard	£5 10s.
To 36 of kersey at 2s. 6d.	£4 4s.
To 19½ of plain cloth at 2s. 6d.	£2 8s. 9d.
To two gross of coat buttons at 21d. per gross	8s. 6d.
To three gross of breast buttons	3s.
To one dozen skins at 5½d. per piece peck	5s. 6d.
To 7½ yards of coloured fustian at 10d. per yard for pockets for the waistcoats	6s. 3d.
To 2lb. of thread at 2s. per pound	4s.
To half a gross of hooks and eyes	6d.
To 3 pieces of stay tape	9d.
To 34 ells of Russia cloth at 5d. per ell to line the waistcoats and breeches	17s.
To line the waistcoats and breeches	14s. 6d.
To one pound of thread	2s.
To 7½ yards of Dutch check at 1s. 10d. per yard for handkerchiefs	13s. 9d.
To 9¾ yards of garlic Holland at 16d. per yard for neckcloths	13s.
Per one ell of garlic Holland per neck	1s. 6d.
	————
	£16 13s.

30. [p. 34] Brought forwards | £18 0s. 1d.
19 May 1712

To 23 hats bought of Thomas Pittflow	£2 6s.
To shoe buckles	3s. 4d.
To 8 pair of shoes of George Byard	19s.
To 9 pair of shoes of Abraham Allin	£1 1s.
To 10 pair of shoes of Edward Atterwood	£1 0s. 5d.
To 3½ yards of Russia cloth at 4d. per yard	1s. 2d.
To 24 pair stockings for the boys	£2 3s. 6d.
To Richard James per making 13 suits	£3 12s.
To Jonathan . . . Edwards making 11 suits	£3 0s. 6d.
To shirts and shifts	£1 14s. 8¾d.
To one hat, 2s.; handkerchiefs, 6d.; gloves, 6d.; shoes, 1s. 10d. for Elkanah Sunderland	4s. 10d.
	————
	£34 6s. 3¾d.

31. 9 May

To 5 pairs of gloves for the girls	2s.	11d.
To buckles for the girls		6d.
To 1½ yard of glazed Holland, 17d.; per tape, 1s.; whalebone, 1s.; silk, 2d.; thread & galloon, 4d.; buckram and canvas	4s.	8d.

31 May

To 7 yards of black silk for hoods, 13s.	£1 1s.	
To 4 pair of bodices at 4s. 3d. per pair	17s.	
To 5 silk laces and silk to make the hoods	2s.	
To 5 pairs of clogs for the girls	2s.	8d.
To making 4 mantuas and petticoats	6s.	
To two pieces of serge for the girls' gowns & petticoats with 3 yards of shalloon per borders	£3 15s.	6d.
To 5 pairs of stockings for girls	8s.	
	£41 6s.	9¾d.

32. 18 October

To sundry necessaries for clothing Rebecca Woodstock viz	3s.	9½d.
To 24 of Russia cloth yards		[blank]
To 1½ yards of black silk for a hood	4s.	3d.
To two ells of Holland at 21d. per ell	3s.	6d.
To 3 quarters & $\frac{2}{16}$ of genting	1s.	6d.
To one pair of gloves, 7d.; a pair stocking 16d.	1s.	11d.
To clogs & pattens, 17d.; and one pair of buckles, 3d.	1s.	8d.
	£42 3s.	5¼d.

33. [p. 35] Brought forwards

1713	£42 3s.	5¼d.
To making gown petticoat and body lining	3s.	
To making a cloth petticoat		6d.
	£42 6s.	11¼d.

34. 27 October

To 2½ yards of Dutch check at 2s. 9d. per yard aprons	£4 4s.	2d.
To ½ yard $\frac{1}{16}$ of Holland per handkerchiefs	1s.	1d.
31 October To a baize petticoat	2s.	4d.
3 November To one yard of damask for stays	2s.	2d.
4 November To one yard of Russia cloth		5d.
6 November To a pair of stays, 8s.; lace, 3d.; girdle, 6d.	8s.	9¾d.
To a bonnet		6d.
To tape for aprons		6d.
To one pair of shoes	1s.	6d.
To another pair of shoes	1s.	8d.
	£43 10s.	1d.

19

35. 15 May 1713

To 26 new hats bought of Thomas Pittflow	£2	12s.	
To 20 Holland caps for girls	£1		
19 August			
To 14 yards of cloth for boys' breeches at 5s. 6d.	£3	17s.	
To 24 yards of linen cloth to line the breeches		14s.	
To three ells of canvas		2s.	3d.
To 1½lb. of thread, 3s. 4d.; and one piece of stay tape, 3d.		3s.	7d.
To making 25 pairs of boys' breeches at 16d. per pair	£1	13s.	4d.
To skins for pockets for the breeches		6s.	6d.
Per one gross of the best sort of leather buttons		2s.	6d.
To one pair of new shoes		2s.	4d.
	£54	3s.	7d.

36.

To sundry necessaries Rebecca Woodstock			10d.
To mending two pair of shoes		1s.	8d.
To Dowlass for shifts		7s.	6d.
To Holland for Rebecca Woodstock			6d.
To . . . two pair of stockings for ditto		3s.	
To three pairs of gloves for the same			8d.
	£54	16s.	11d.
Rests undispersed of the legacy	£45	3s.	1d.
	£100	0s.	

37. [p. 36] Memorandum.

29 September 1716 the neat stock including £809 10s. 4½d. dead stock &c.	£1554	16s.	1d.
25 March 1712 neat stock including dead stock &c.	£1495	16s.	2d.

The income from the meetings, yarn mops, stable interest, rent &c (as appears plain in the accounts) has exceeded the expense in provision, rent, wages, taxes, repairs &c in four years & 6 months time; the difference being   £58 19s. 11d.

And received since 25 March 1712 in legacies and subscriptions to 29 September 1716	£783	18s.	10¾d.
	£842	18s.	9¾d.
Received since 29 September 1716 in legacies	£333	6s.	8d.
	£1176	5s.	5¾d.

From 29 September 1712 to 29 September 1716 ʌe boys' earnings including the profit of the yarn &c comes to	£567	2s.	6¾d.
& the profit amounts to	£190	2s.	9d.
The earnings amounts to &c	£376	19s.	9¾d.

There appears to be lost from the first settlement to the year 1712 upwards £1019 3s. 10d. and about 17 children put out apprentice. And to the year 1716, 26 children have been out out.

38. [p. 37] From our monthly meeting at the Peel, London, 27 March 1717.

To the friends and brethren at the monthly meeting at Cork or elsewhere in Ireland.

Dear Friends,

Whereas our friend Daniel Cooper having acquainted us of his intention, if the Lord permit, to remove himself & family to reside in your city and requesting a certificate of the conversations while amongst us:

Therefore these are to certify whom it may concern that after due enquiry made concerning them we do not find but they have been of sober and orderly conversation during their residence amongst us. And we sincerely desire the Lord's comfortable presence may accompany these our friends and that they may be preserved in the blessed truth to the end of . . . their days.

So dear friends in the salutation of brotherly love, we remain your friends and brethren in the fellowship of the gospel of peace.

Signed as above, written by us.

39. [p. 38] It is ordered that all the children come down (at meal times) together as soon as called and sit down at the table orderly; keeping silence and not any to go from the table on any account whatsoever. And if anything be wanting one to stand up and speak modestly to their master or mistress or any that may be there to have the care over them. And none to carry porringers, spoons or any thing else into the kitchen or pantry; only such as may be ordered so to do. That no boy or girl talk of any thing they hear or see in the workroom, school or family, either abroad or to the ancient friends or servants of the house.

That no boy or girl strike each other with their hands, sticks or any thing else, but in case of provocation immediately to acquaint the steward thereof or some other in his absence.

That no boy or girl direct each other in their cyphering without leave from the master.

That no boy or girl complain of their victuals, work, schooling or one of another or anything else to any person out of the house or in the family, but to acquaint the steward therewith.

40. [p. 39] Clause of Elizabeth Pentlebury's will bearing date 3 April 1708.

Memorandum. That it is my mind and will that my house which is in Pennington Street and [which] in my last will, bearing equal date with this, I have given after the expiration of seven years, from the first quarter day that shall be next after my decease or [upon the] death of Henry Worster if that happen before the expiration of the seven years, unto John Field of London, haberdasher, for him to dispose of as he or his executors, administrators or assignees shall see meet, shall be disposed of by him or them or the rents or profits thereof for the remainder of the lease of ninety-nine years that shall be unexpired for and towards the relief of the poor at the workhouse of the people called Quakers near Clerkenwell, and that he or they shall assign over the said house to the overseers thereof as the Six Weeks Meeting of the said people in London shall direct for the benefit only of the said poor. In witness whereof I have hereunto set my hand this twenty third day of the second month called April, 1708.

Witness   E:P the mark of Elizabeth Pentlebury
John Field

41. Memorandum.

I spoke with friends about the house the Widow Pentlebury left unto John Field after seven years if the son of one Worster lived so long.

Now there are 4 of the 7 years to come and the mother and Widow Pentlebury's son are willing friends should have it if they'll advance ten pounds.

But now the son refuseth.

42. [p. 40] A Copy of a letter from Francis Hope's mother.

My Dear Children,   Yarmouth, 19 May 1717

I have your letter before me, which I am very much troubled to see the case so much altered with you since . . . your father left you; for you told him you were well done by and did not want for anything, which makes me to strange that in so small a time you should be so hardly used. What is thy master worse for thy father's being kind to him? What was the reason John was so whipped and beat with a cane, or what had he done? Let me know. Why did not you let your uncle John know, that he might have taken care about you, for you shall not be hardly used if that I do but know it. Thy Father intends to write to your uncle John about you. Frank, I am not pleased . . . [that] thee should write so as you intend . . . to go out of the workhouse. Where would you go to seek your living, or what could you do? Thy talking so is a means to displease all thy friends. Thou told thy father that thou had a mind to learn all that thy master could learn thee in arithmetic; and as soon as thou is fit for business we intend to take thee home. Therefore mind and do not displease thy best friends. I pray God give you grace to fear him and then you will be good boys, so shall I have comfort in you. So my dear children let me hear from you how things go with you, for if your master be not kind to you, you shall be put to some place else. If that you had let thy Uncle John know, he would not a suffered you to have been abused no more, but I hope to hear better from you. I remain your very loving mother.

Your father and sisters hath all their loves to you.

                                                        Rachael Lindley

Why did thou send thy letter unsealed direct for Amor Lindley Merchant in Yarmouth?

43. [p. 41] 30 January 1716, memorandum.

Having occasion to desire Elizabeth Rand to clean two pairs of the boys' breeches she had neglected two or three weeks, she answered she would not, neither would she carry them out of the room though desired. Saying, as she was paid for wherefore should she do more than they. I told her the meetings required everyone in this house to be helpful according to their ability, and she being an able woman, the committee for her encouragement had given her something for so doing. To which she slightingly answered, ah, four shillings for a whole year, and bid me do my worst and turn her out as soon as I would, for she would not stay if she begged her bread from door to door, but she would not go till the cold weather was gone. She talking, or rather scolding both loud and fast in a passionate way of expression, the girls being in the same room at the same time at breakfast, it was to them a bad example. And upon signifying to her the end of friends' charity to poor friends, here was answered, as they were thankful and willing to assist one another according to their ability and occasion required, she told me, she received no charity but worked hard for her maintenance and at many times saith she has not so much as she deserves considering her service in the house; and saith, she is a mother in the family notwithstanding her ill example to the children & unwillingness to assist the aged or helpless unless when and how she pleases. And having let a wrong mind so much prevail scarce anything of diet I give her (though at her request other ways than the bill of [fare] directs) pleaseth, but some reflection will be cast as if the poor had not sufficient. And in a very unhandsome manner said to me, holding up her hands in the public workroom at breakfast, my heart pities those poor creatures that are under thy care, for thou wilt pinch them.

And such treatment as this we meet with often from her, especially when we desire anything of her for the service of the house, which I have borne long with as some friends of her quarter know. But for the quiet of the family & the good of the children who hear the authority of the house frequently undervalued, which is a great hindrance to their education:

We desire the committee would please to use their authority discouraging such disorderly spirits, who are so resolutely bent, if their wasteful humours are not answered, to run down and make void all manner of government in the family, which we think is very hard on us who have given our bond to the [p. 42] committee. And also our reputation lies at stake for honest discharge of our trust under you. And there being several who upon slight occasions have given us the like treatment, which we have cause to think is the more by the example and strengthening each other.

There was disorderly persons in the house when we first came, yet they were so prudently dealt with as that I never heard (as I remember) such unhandsome expressions as from some now in this house, nor so slightly valued the committee and monthly meetings.

And when the maids don't please Elizabeth Rand she calls them proud saucy sluts and saith they're upheld in it.

And sometimes she calls some of the children to evidence for her, and if they do not speak just as she would have them, she fiercely calls them wicked lying children and saith they are countenanced in it.

She told my husband, Haman built a gallows for Mordica and was hanged on it himself.

23

This as near as could be remembered, as a great deal more which for brevity sake I omit.

44. Her acknowledgement to the committee.

I, having some time since been charitably provided for at friends' workhouse with a comfortable maintenance, did not put such a value thereon as I am now sensible I ought to have done. But by my disorderly behaviour and ill example became an exercise to the government of the family, so that for the peace of the house the committee were obliged to discharge me the same. All which I willingly and openly acknowledge and am sorry for my said misbehaviours, desiring friends would favourably accept this, my acknowledgement and that it may be read in the said family as caution to them. And I humbly request the committee would please to admit me the house again and desire through the Lord's assistance to be of a more peaceable behaviour and better example for the time to come. Witness my hand this 12th day of July 1717.

In the Cyprus Box   Elizabeth Rand, her
amongst the bills   mark was ER.
the original of this paper.

45. [p. 43] To the adjourned meeting at the Bull and Mouth, 10 July 1717. Hearing that [it] is proposed . . . Elizabeth Rand . . . come to this house and understanding that she is not willing to accept thereof unless she can have relief no other way, and that I and my wife will come under some engagement that she should be better used than formerly; to which I have this to observe to the meeting, that when she was here she had privileges that none (that I know of) have had the like before. She being helpful in the family at her first coming and . . . seemed content . . . we were kind to her in many respects & had more money given her as encouragement than any poor friend in the house, but after some time she began to set a great value upon her service and what money was given her by the committee or otherways she looked upon far short of what she deserved. What our provision is, is generally known, with which she was not easy, though my wife did . . . endeavour to please her by not keeping her to the bill of fare as the rest of the poor friends were. And as to the business she did we can easily make it appear it was inconsiderable, so that she spent a great part of her time in walking abroad, and would frequently go out and come in in a resolute frame of mind contrary to the orders of the house, which introduced a liberty & disorder in the same which with her undue and frequent provocations and bad behaviour was a great disadvantage in the family, especially amongst the children (who ought not to hear and see they who have the care over them lessened in their authority) who we find by experience should have better examples. Those circumstances considered, we are careful lest she may prove a more troublesome woman than formerly if she be admitted again contrary to her inclinations and upon her own terms, and thereby render herself unworthy of so good a provision as this house, be an ill example to the family & an exercise to us. From your loving friend.

Workhouse, 10 July 1717   Richard Hutton

We are not at all against her coming in again if the meeting and the committee, who have seen her behaviour think well of it. Would she be of a better behaviour for the time to come?

46. [p. 44] Memorandum.

Note: the gain of the wool account and interest of the stock in the treasurer's hands hath exceeded the same for the year 1715 by upwards of £84, which is the occasion of the advance of yarn &c. And the moderate price of bread and few repairs the occasion of not running out the £84.

Sending in a great many children, we conclude, would be a great encouragement to benefactors. Especially when they see the numbers and good order increase in the house.

There has been given within this two years by sundry benefactors about £800. And it may be observed that in the first ten years to the year 1712 only seventeen boys were put out apprentice, but since 1712, to 1716, 26 children have been put out.

It's our opinion it would be great advantage to the youth of this family if the ancient friends were strictly charged by their respective monthly meetings from whence they are sent into the house, that they forbear all murmuring, contention and that the plain language be faithfully kept to by them, and that they may willingly be subject to the orders of the committee and not to carry reports out of the house that tend to lessening so good a provision in any branch of it. And as these great disadvantages are removed we hope to find it much easier to bring our children up in that innocence and good order which faithful friends desire they may be brought into, and preserved in. Which satisfaction we desire friends may have, who have willingly and cheerfully gone through the great charge and labour in their tender care. For preserving the youth of their poor brethren and sisters, whose children as they grow up in a sense of the holy truth may prove serviceable in a succeeding generation . . . we do believe is all that is in the view of &c.

47. [p. 45] Directions for the school master.

1. That he is hired as a servant and . . . is expected his whole time be employed in the service of the house, and that he carefully keep the accounts or what part of them the steward may require.

2. And that he be diligent in school time in order to let the children have time to do their work, play &c and attend the children out of school time or when at work, in case the man that looks after them be otherwise engaged that the children may be kept out of disorder and make good work.

3. And that he shun too much familiarity with the family, also to discourage whispering or any disorder therein whereby he may be serviceable in keeping up the reputation of the house.

48. [p. 46: Blank in the original.]

49. [p. 47] Balance   47 debtor
29 September 1717
To sundry accounts being debts due to the house
and goods remaining therein with cash in hand.

3 – To rent of the tenements 224:225:226:227:228:		£20	5s.
3 – To Devonshire House Monthly Meeting	2 quarters	£35 10s.	10d.
3 – To Bull and Mouth	3 quarters	£41 11s.	4d.
3 – To the Peel	1 quarter	£14 13s.	11d.
3 – To the Savoy	1	£16 7s.	3½d.
3 – To Ratcliffe	1	£16 6s.	9¾d.
3 – To Horsley Down	1	£7 14s.	
3 – To Particular persons for allowances &c.		£7	8s.
3 – To absentees' box	98	10s.	10d.
9 – To bad debts	205	£39 10s.	4d.
6 – To brewing vessels	336	£34 16s.	4d.
5 – To coals	425	£36 12s.	3d.
2 – To cash remaining in the steward's hands	344	£19 17s.	10½d.
5 – To clothing	426	16s.	10d.
3 – To Hannah Doggett's legacy	277	16s.	8d.
3 – To Denham, a tenant	42	£1	
5 – To house expenses in provision	459	£22 10s.	5d.
3 – To Edward Hayward for mops	317	£1 10s.	11¼d.
1 – To interest of East India & South Sea stock	375	£53	
8 – To legacies not received	11	£120	
7 – To dead stock as formerly	40	£650	
3 – To Katherine Miller for rent	135	£5	5s.
4 – To wool, mops &c.	396	£100	7s.
3 – To meeting of twelve, 6 quarters	327	£110	3s. 11d.
5 – To writing school	382	15s.	
3 – To sewing school	386	£1	7s. 3d.
5 – To stable	367	£3	6s. 4d.
1 – To South Sea & East India stock	368	£1547	2s. 6d.
3 – To Elizabeth Hearn's legacy	341	£4	6s.
		£2952 17s.	3d.

50. [p. 48] Per contra   48
29 September 1717
To sundry accounts owing

Per salary and wages 28:180:79:146:183		£19	7s. 10d.
Per Thomas Coxe's legacy for clothing the children	349	£73 12s.	2½d.
Per house expenses for bread &c.	459	18s.	9d.
Per William Kight for boys' hats, 7 in the chest	229	12s.	10d.
Per John Marlow's legacy	163	£5 11s.	2¾d.
Per Thomas Pixley for butter and cheese	346	£1 19s.	7½d.

26

Per rent of the house	81	£15
Per repairs due to workmen	428	£6 5s. 1d.
Per stable due to the farrier and per gross bill	367	£2 13s.
Per taxes due this day	378	£11 13s.
		£137 13s. 6¾d.
To legacies and subscriptions	474	£1187 5s. 6¾d.
		£1324 19s. 1½d.

51. 1 – In South Sea and East
India stock with interest due £1640 2s. 6d.
2 – In cash remaining the steward's
hands £19 17s. 10¼d.
3 – In debts esteemed good £284 2s. 2¾d.
4 – In wool &c. £100 7s. ½d.
5 – In provision and coals £64 0s. 10½d.
6 – In brewing vessels £34 16s. 4½d.

£2143 6s. 10½d.

7 – In dead stock £650
8 – In legacies not received £120
9 – In bad debts £39 10s. 4½d.

£809 10s. 4½d.

£2952 17s. 3d.

Owing for rent, taxes, repairs &c. £64 1s. 4¾d.
To the remaining part of legacy left
by Thomas Coxe to clothe the children £73 12s. 2d.
Received by legacies and subscriptions £1187 5s. 6¾d.

£1324 19s. 1½d.

Neat stock this 29 September 1717 £1627 18s. 1½d.
Neat stock the 29 September 1716 £1554 16s. 1d.

Clear gains in the year 1717 £73 2s. ½d.

52. [p. 49] We find if the whole time were allotted for spinning they
would have earned (including the profit of the yarn):
Quarterly £16 11s. 6d.
And that they have earned this
present quarter by spinning £10 6s. 6d.
We lost because we did not spin:
Quarterly £6 5s.

4

Lost in one year £25

27

Their earnings at sewing will not defray the charge of the mistress's board and wages by	£9 7s.	½d.
The whole loss by sewing in one year is	£34 7s.	½d.

53. *Two bank bills as follows: William Steel's legacy*

No. 99 Payable to John Miller for fifty pounds on demand.
  Dated 5 October 1717
£50 J. Shrimpton   Joshua Odams

No. 124 Payable to John Miller fifty pounds on demand.
  Dated 5 October 1717
£50 J. Shrimpton   Joshua Odams

54. [p. 50] Memorandum, April 1717 and the seventh day.
When there were several helpful hands in the house and all were taken off from their constant employ in order the able amongst them might have a better opportunity to attend the aged, sick, weak &c, notwithstanding all this, still complaints were carried out of the house: the poor were oppressed, and the sick and aged wanted due tendance. Which proved to the disadvantage of the house by discouraging several poor honest friends who might have been helpful and also thankful for so good and comfortable a provision.

And about that time we had 22 boys 5 girls and the looking after the boys' linen, woollen clothes, washing their rooms, making the beds and combing their heads had been, . . . and then were, done by two of the ancient women who were then able and now by age and weakness are made incapable.

Now we have 50 children, viz: 32 boys and 17 girls [*sic*]. 18 Men and 10 Women who are generally aged and weak, two lame & one blind. Two of them have mostly kept their beds and none of late have been sent into the house, especially women, except such as are scarcely able to help themselves, and but one woman in the house at this time that can stir about well and in many respects she very unfit for a nurse.

55. [p. 51: a rough draft of item **61**.]

56. [p. 52] To [blank] Monthly Meeting &c.
Dear friends,   9 June 1717
The ancient friend recommended by minute from your monthly meeting dated [blank], to be taken into friends' workhouse was this day before us who appeared in a very weak condition and under several infirmities, as he saith, unable to help himself without assistance. And the able in this house not being sufficient to help and attend the aged and weak already here at such times when weakness or sickness happens, we therefore cannot admit him unless the meeting would please to send some able friend into the house with him for his attendance. Otherways he may want necessary assistance, and may prove hurtful to the reputation of the house.

57. Kind steward,

These are to acquaint thee that I am safe arrived at my uncle's house where I was kindly received. My love to thee and thy wife, also to all the friends of the committee and to my master that taught me to write. My love to all the ancient friends and all the children of the workhouse which were my school fellows. And I should be very glad to hear of any of their welfare, as well as for my own. I thank thee and the committee for all I have received. My uncle is about placing me at Exeter to Arthur Purchas, a tucker. I am in all due respects thy friend,

Keyford, 30 October 1717   Thomas Sands

58. [p. 53] To friends of the quarterly meeting, both men & women. Dear friends,

We being under a sense of the great providence of God to us and of your kindness, whom he hath made instrumental in making so necessary a provision for us in our old age, where we are eased and disentangled from those cares & difficulties which several of our circumstances formerly laid us under; we are willing to make this acknowledgement in gratitude that you may be more encouraged to continue your favours . . . to such others as hereafter age and poverty may bring into such a necessitous condition, none knowing what disappointments may reduce them to.

We do verily believe that in no private lodgings we can be so cheap and so easily provided for with the same accommodation as we have in this hospital. Whilst in particular lodgings there are many things that we must do for ourselves, . . . here [they] may be done for us.

For in such lodgings we must have been penned up in less room and not so airy. And we find this house is very well situated, affording us good airy rooms, several of us having had our health much better since we came here than we had before.

Also if any friends remain dissatisfied with this house we desire they would come and see the manner and order [of] it and those objects of charity that are in it. We hoping their frequent visiting of us would dissipate their offences.

We did lately hear that some persons of note did come to visit us and see the ordering of our family and were well satisfied, and reported things were better than they had been informed.

We conceive it would be for a more general information and satisfaction if the women friends would please to have a meeting here once a month, or some times when they think fit, whose oversight and advice may be of service to some in this house and family.

[p. 54] We are several of us aged men & women, some of us fourscore years old and upwards, and here are 28 boys and 12 girls employed in work, as well as taught to read and write and cast accounts, whom we hope to prove useful men and women in the succeeding age, answerable to the care and charge you are at for them.

Also here are two meetings a week, first days & fifth days in the mornings, which is a great privilege and benefit to our family and especially to the aged, and is of service to strangers that frequently come to our meetings, we being well visited by public friends.

29

And now dear friends, with humble acknowledgement of your great care and kindness to us, we conclude and do rest and remain your very thankful poor brethren & gifters in our measures of truth.

The Women	John Heywood
Mary Cockbill	Benjamin Antrobus
Martha Sands	John Harper
Elizabeth Joans	Thomas Priest
Mary Smith	Richard Smart
Elizabeth Rand	Thomas Portland
Elizabeth Beadle	Edward Clark
Mary Lawrence	Thomas Waite
Joane Miles	Daniel Rosier
Margrat Clark	Richard Heywood
Dorothy Straham	

This is a copy of a paper delivered to the Quarterly Meeting at Devonshire House December 1713.

59. [p. 55] Memorandum about the poor working in the house &c.

1st It seems not to be consistent with the orders of the committee to give liberty to friends in this house to work for themselves.

2d It prevents their assisting each other in times of weakness.

3d It gives opportunity to go or send in and about the town more than may be convenient, and cannot be easily prevented their managing business being for an excuse.

4th When there were many ancient friends in the house who were able and helpful, then working and tending each other was thought an oppression, upon which the work was all laid aside in order to give better opportunity at that time to be serviceable to each other, though there were 34 aged people about 29 children to look after and mend for &c.

5th And now there are but 20 ancient friends who are mostly aged and weak, one blind and another lame who has kept his bed about six months together and come not down stairs in that time as we know of, and now we have 49 children, 17 of them girls, and takes up both time and care to keep them in order as combing, washing, mending linen &c.

6th It hath been the inclination of some friends in the house to work for themselves, but the orders of the committee and the design of the house being so contrary to their desire, and as they were made sensible of it, put a stop to any public practice thereof.

7th And may discourage others from coming into the house they imagining the allowance of the house not to be sufficient, hearing the poor already in the house are allowed to work to supply themselves with what they may suppose the house doth not allow.

8th And the committee having allowed what the quarterly meeting judges sufficient in diet and lodging and the monthly meetings find clothes, and several small helps in money given them by diverse hands, makes less occasion to cumber themselves and the house by laying tasks upon themselves to so little purpose.

60. [p. 56] A copy &c.

Yet, every[one] in this case should take prudent care that an injury do not make them lose their temper, and draw them into an indecency and so betray them into a discovery either of a weak judgement or intemperate passions; that they do not help to destroy a reputation which the false accusations of their enemies could never hurt if they had not lent them their own assistance. When they betray perverseness and ill humour, a morose nature and a revengeful temper . . . they are sure to meet with scorn instead of respect, whereas if under the severest provocations a man can preserve that kindness and humanity which shall add a reputation to his other abilities, and use no other severity than what a just defence makes necessary, he has an opportunity to show the brightest character, that he is completely master of himself and of his own conduct, that he knows what he should be, and yet more knows how to be what he should. This must heighten a man's reputation with his friends and force an inward respect even from enemies themselves.

61. [p. 57] Memorandum, workhouse the 31 December 1717.

At the time the children were clothed they were 49 in number, and 31 of them were clothed at the charge of Thomas Coxe's legacy, they being maintained at the direct charge of the monthly meetings. The other 18 of them were, most of them, clothed by their parents and friends who generally were satisfied to be at the charge themselves. And upon examination we conclude that 8 of the said 18 children must have fallen to the same charge with [the] first 31 had not the parents of some and the relations of others taken the same upon themselves. So . . . the case of them runs almost parallel with this now depending.

Please to consider, if this case be made a precedent and admitted to after the method of clothing agreed to by the committee, as being supposed to differ but little from being directly at the charge of the monthly meeting, if there may not be room and there is occasion to suppose it's intended for others to apply who esteem themselves to have . . . [the same] right and expect the same privileges as much as others may do from them, and so the first being admitted to open a way for a second and lastly for all without distinction. And thereby the charity which might have been intended for the ease of the monthly meetings' charge will be bestowed for the advantage of particular persons of whom some seem to be in good ability.

We intend no profit to the house by not clothing all the children without distinction, but to save about £32 for the monthly meetings' use, of which about £10 16s. would have been laid out for the clothing of such children whose friends seem to be in good ability as is before observed.

Particulars

Devonshire house: Thomas Sands*, W. Sanson*, Francis Hope, John Hope, Jacob Pritty.

Peel: Sam Richards*, Daniel Foster*, Jacob Foster*, Mary Henderkin*, Joseph Ladson, Joseph Read, Richard Everingham, John Ansel, Joseph Ansel, Sarah Isaac, John Love.

Southwark: Thomas Robins*, in all 18.

62. [p. 58] Dear kinsman, Leek, 10 December 1717. This is the second time I have set to write to thee. Both my hands and eyes sometimes fail me that I cannot do as I would, yet, I thank the Lord, am content. I received thy lines sometimes since and was glad of it, but was sorry that thy wife continues indisposed. I had a letter from thy father a little before I had thine, did not hear but they were all pretty well. I am often suddenly ill. I take it to be the companion of old age. I have been six months at home, save in Chester two weeks. I am like to be at home the reversion of the winter – if I do live, which I sometimes question. As in times of suffering, I never feared them, nor do I fear death. Three things I have desired with submission, to wit: a short visitation, my understanding, and an easy passage. Now dear cousin I seem weary with this short scribble. Remember me to friends who would be too many to name, also to John Bills and his good wife, and I conclude in the same to thee and thine in which I am thy loving uncle.

William Tallowfield

My love also to friends at Ware.

63. 25 December 1718.

Coming into the house I had in cash.	£17	I have in cash	£2 17s.
		Bought in a stow grate	£1 14s.
Since disposed on in household goods &c.	£3	Also a clock	£4 10s.
		A watch	£5
Received 6 years interest . . .	£21 12s.	Interest	£21 12s.
		Goods &c a cupboard	£2 7s.
	£41 12s.		£38
		Loss	£3 12s.
			£41 12s.

64. [p. 59] Memorandum, 31 December 1717.

John Conyers and John Gorden came to our meeting at the Peel this day and after the meeting followed the children home. Came not in but stayed near the tenements. And we being come home and the door shut, I went from home again and as I was passing by where they were standing, John Conyers called and asked me where I was going. I told him, about a little business. He said, I want to speak with thee but I suppose thou has not time. I told him, I had time to answer any reasonable question. Then said he, I want to know how Elizabeth Gorden behaves herself in the house. I considered a little, and desired to know of him if he was sent by order of the meeting to enquire. He said, no matter for that, I can tell the meeting if I please. I told him short, I would not tell him anything of her behaviour. So he seemed to go away very much displeased and threatening said, I will tell of thee then.

This is what passed at that bout, and as soon as I had acquainted my wife what had past, somebody knocked at the door. My wife went and opened the door and John Conyer and John Gorden were both there, and John Conyer said, where is thy husband. Did thou not see him but just now? He made no answer to that, but said, where is Elizabeth Gorden? I want to speak with her. My wife told him, she came from her home but yesterday and she came but now from the meeting, and further said, I know no business thou hast with her. Therefore don't intend thou shalt see her. Then he began to be more troublesome, and I coming out of the parlour desired him to go about his business, and told him, we would not be thus insulted. He thereupon called aloud and said, thou art in a passion, and now I see you are guilty. You'll not let me see the girl. But I will tell the meeting, and threatened much, saying, you tell John Constantine your stories but John Constantine may not always rule the meeting. I told him he was a saucy boy & bid him go about his business and asked him if John Gorden had given him a pocket full of apples for coming this errand. He said, we were but servants and maintained by friends. I told him, we were servants, but not his servant. He said, he was a member of the meeting and came on the meeting's business, and said aloud, you are impudent, several times over, standing in the house, and went out of the door calling aloud as he went along the alley, you are impudent and friends maintain you and I will give the meeting an account of you.

65. [p. 60] Short sentences worthy of serious consideration and a good application. Being the meditations of R.G. when at sea, the 9th of the first month called March 1717.

Tis man's contemplative felicity to converse in his thoughts with that glory which is prepared for those that die, so as to live eternally.

True wisdom crowns all the accomplishments of man, but tis a flower which grows not in nature's garden; and great is their number who might have attained true wisdom, had they not already thought themselves too wise.

Grace is a bud, which in the summer of eternity becomes a flower of glory. Grace is a stream, flowing from the fountain of divine love. Serious meditations are the conduits through which this celestial stream flows to the soul.

Holy affections are the cisterns wherein the soul is bathed with heavenly joys. Heavenly joys are the springs of life flowing from Christ the fountain of life, which alone can satisfy the appetite of a thirsty soul.

The soul, being a spiritual substance, requires spiritual food. Therefore, all elementary bodies being contrary to its nature fall short of giving it the least nourishment, for every animal receives nutriment from that which is coherent with its own nature.

As the soul cannot partake of such nourishment that is not homogenial to its spirituality, so neither can it be the receptacle of any pollution by any thing that is contrary to its essentiality, for the soul being a spirit, can receive neither good, nor evil, by anything that's inanimate or corporeal.

They who enjoy not the God of love cannot obtain the love of God, for our love of God is nothing but our reflection of God's love to us. So that, till God is pleased to love us, our love can never please him.

God being the first and the last in the great world, it's our duty to make him so in the little world (viz. man). Practise therefore to make Him thy last thoughts at night when thou sleepest and thy first in the morning when thou wakest. So shall thy fancy be sanctified in the night and thy understanding rectified in the day. Then shall thy rest be peaceful, thy labour prosperous, thy life pious & thy death glorious.

[p. 61] Love thy neighbour for God's sake, and God for thy sake, and [be] redeemed . . . for his mercy's sake. If thy love hath any other object, it is false love. If thy object have any other end, it is self-love.

Things temporal are sweeter in the expectation than in the fruition. Things eternal are sweeter in the fruition than in the expectation. Vain is that journey whose end affords less pleasure than the way to it.

Tis an evil knowledge to know that thou shouldst embrace, unless thou likewise embrace the good thou knows. The breath of divine knowledge is the bellows of divine love; and the flame of divine love is the perfection of knowledge.

If thou are not willing that thy time should pass too fast thou must beware of using too much pastime, for thy life of voluptuousness blazeth away like a taper in the wind. The blast of honour waste it, and the heat of pleasure melts it.

How much the more any person delights in sensual pleasure, so much the less he enjoys of heavenly pleasure.

In all outward calamities, tis necessary . . . we should eye the hand that sent them, and the sin for which they were sent . . . If we thankfully receive the message, he that sent it will discharge the messenger, but whilst we delight in the pleasure of sin, we must of necessity taste the bitterness of misery.

If thou desire rest to thy soul, be just, fear not to suffer injury. Tis the unjust mind that is always in labour, for it . . . practises the evil it hath projected to avoid the evil it hath deserved.

If thou desires knowledge, examine the end of thy desire. Is it only to know, then tis curiosity; is it because thou mayst be known, then it is vanity; but because thou mayst edify, it is charity; if because thou mayst be edified, it is wisdom: for that knowledge turns to excrement that hath not some heat of divine wisdom to digest it.

If thou findst thy self ignorant, be not ashamed to learn, for he that is so fondly modest not to acknowledge his own defects of knowledge shall in time be foully impudent to justify his ignorance. [p. 62] And as ignorance is the greatest of all infirmities, if justified, the chiefest of all follies.

If any one hath wounded thee with injuries, meet him with patience. Hasty words rankle the wound, soft language dresses it, forgiving cures it, forgetfulness takes away the scar. Tis more noble by silence to avoid an injury, than by argument to overcome it, for much arguing doth oftentimes kindle the sparks of contention into a flame of revenge.

At whatsoever time thou dost remember thy sins without grief, so often thou repeatest thy sins for not grieving. He that will not mourn for the evil he hath done gives earnest for the evil he intends to do. Nothing can assuage that fire which sin hath made, but only that water which repentance hath drawn.

Let the ground of all thy religious actions be obedience, which is better than sacrifice. True religion consists rather of well doing than opinion. So the question is not whether this or that opinion be right, but whether the conversation be good, for such as we sow so shall we reap.

Be not unstable in thy resolutions, nor various in thy actions, nor inconsistent in thy affections, but use deliberation, lest thou repent the acting of what thy resolved and knit such a knot in thy affections which thou canst . . . have loosed. Consider therefore what thou dost resolve, that thou mayst without sorrow perform thy resolution.

Let not the profits, pleasures or honours of this world dispossess thee of the enjoyments of the other world. Consider that all momentary enjoyments pass away as soon as received, the other, once received, never passeth away.

Keep thy soul in action, lest her faculties rust for want of motion. To eat, sleep, or sport too long stops the natural course of . . . her natural actions. To dwell too long in the employments of the body is both the cause and sign of a dull spirit.

Consider what thou wert, what thou art, and what thou shall be. Also consider what's within thee, what's above thee, what's beneath thee, what's against thee, what was before thee, and what shall be after thee. This will bring to thyself humility, to thy neighbour charity, to the world contempt, and to thy God true obedience. By these considerations thou shalt be able to see through most things in the world.

[p. 63] Let not a good intention flatter thee in a bad action, for what is essentially evil no circumstance can make good; matters not with what mind thou dost that which being done is unlawful. If thy act be good thy intention crowns it. If bad, it deposes thy intention. In short, no evil action can be well done.

In thy discourse take heed what thou speakest, to whom thou speakest, how thou speakest, what thou speakest. Speak truly. When thou speakest, speak wisely. A fool's heart is in his tongue, but a wise man's tongue is in his heart.

66. For Mr Richard Hutton, 31 March 1718.
Sir,
This day I was informed that the children under your care have not a sufficient allowance of food to fill their bellies . . . I am sorry that such a report should be raised among your people for I did think you always took the best of care amongst your poor. Children are hungry and growing and require more food, but hungry bellies and cold water betwixt meals do not agree, and raising them at five a clock in . . . the morning and making them work without their clothes is very hard for children to bear. If the allowance is too little there ought to be complaint made to the committee. I know none of the committee or else I would lay it before them. I have the care of a great many children myself and my comfort is I discharge a good conscience to them. I desire you to look into those things for fear there should come a sickness among them.

67. [p. 64] Loving friend,   Thorncoomb 25 April 1718.
I received thine of the 19th instant, which brought us very unwelcome news concerning the trouble my son and daughter are involved in. The grief it hath occasioned amongst us is scarce to be expressed. My son concealed it from us when in the country so that it was the greater

surprise. The sorrowful tidings which we had not long ago, filled us with . . . grief, but this exceeds it, her death (I mean my daughter Mary) being what we are liable to sooner or later. But, that my son should be so unkind to a sister that ever had too great respect for him as to ruin herself, is hard to be borne. I did, according to thy desire (though unwilling, being sure of a flat denial), show thy letter to their uncles who are worth a great deal as is supposed, and no child, the younger no wife. I was with them and my wife also, which is their own sister, but all in vain, my son, they reflect upon for former miscarriages and blame him for this also (i.e.) for bringing his sister into trouble. She they seem to pity and that's all the assistance they will afford whatever the event be. I am sorry I can send thee no better answer. For my part I am not able to do anything in it. If I were I should readily do it. Tell my daughter Elizabeth we are all pretty well, only we are troubled to think of the calamity [that] may come on them. Give the remembrance of our kind love to yours, also with my kind love to self, I rest.

Thy loving friend,
Samuel Sprak

68. [p. 65] Some observations &c.

It may be observed that in the first ten years of this house's settlement the improvement of the stock and income from the monthly meetings were not sufficient to defray the expense of the house by £1200, which is £120 per year, and about 17 children were put out apprentices within that time, whereby the principal stock became lessened from year to year to the discouragement of benefactors. Which, with the many lessening reports spread abroad in reference to the orders, diet, work &c, has generally hindered its improvement. It may also be observed that as the stock was lessened £120 a year from year to year as aforesaid, so for this 5 or 6 last year past the stock is almost £2000 advanced and 42 put out in that time. Also the income on such a settlement as to amount unto about £100 a year more than the ordinary expense and legacies frequently happening, doth advance the stock yet more. And though there are not so many ancient friends as formerly to live on this plentiful provision, experience showing they are more content with a little managed after their own inclinations and in private & provided by themselves than greater plenty which may come more nearly under the observations of a family, yet the house is better filled with children to whom it is an extraordinary advantage. But, the number of children not increasing this 4 or 5 years last past is the occasion of this memorandum. For we find their sober education and habit of industry renders them more acceptable to masters than children who have not such advantage. So that often times there are more children sought after for apprentices than are in the house of bigness to put out. We suppose the reason why children are so slowly sent in is because so many false reports are carried about and received tending to the discouragement of poor friends who might willingly place their children here were they sensible how naturally children are contented to be doing what they see all their fellows employed about (as experience doth daily show). Such parents conclude the orders of the house are not indulgent enough and thereby prevent their children's education and themselves the advantage of having their [p. 66] children maintained at so low a price as 12d. per week. There has lately been many false stories spread abroad to the defaming of the house and those who have the care thereof and hurt of the children already here, to whom such reports have been privately brought. Which to prevent for the future we see no way at present . . . unless . . . a minute . . . from the committee be . . . directed to each monthly meeting requesting such reports may be discouraged so often as they are related. And also that at the taking children into the house the parents have both orders and bill of fare read to them and report thereof made to the committee before such child be admitted into the house and that no child be taken in who is not willing or cannot comply with both orders and bill of fare.

69. Note: the countenances of the children show they have no want of victuals and their work is no more than what they may finish . . . against dinner time (which several of them doth an hour or two sooner than dinner), having the afternoon for learning and play.

70. The director of the orphan house at Halle in Germany, without any stock (or knowledge of any), built an house and since much enlarged it, wherein are maintained [blank] persons; begun in the year 1696.

71. This house having been regulated by much industry . . . of the most noted amongst friends (as appears by the first minute book), having £1888 subscribed towards it, . . . after 17 years continuance hath 75 persons maintained in it (including steward & servant). May 1718.

72. [p. 67] Memorandum from 1712 &c.

About seven years since there were several helpful hands in the house who were taken from their work they were then employed in, that the able amongst them should have better opportunity to attend the aged, sick and weak. But notwithstanding this, still complaints were carried out of the house that the poor were oppressed, the aged and sick wanted due tendance. Which complaints were a disadvantage to the house in discouraging friends from coming in who might have been helpful and likewise thankful for so comfortable a provision . . . About this time there was in the house about 22 [boys] & 4 girls and the looking after the children's linen and woollen clothes, washing their chambers, making their beds, combing the children's heads &c had been and then were done by two of the ancient women who then were able and now by reason of age and weakness are grown incapable.

And now we have in the house about 28 [boys] and 17 girls, 11 men and 11 women. Two of them, a man and the other a woman, are lame and use crutches, and another woman friend is blind. The rest are mostly aged and weak, of whom several have kept their beds pretty much this last winter and three of the women friends who are usually sent into the house now are not of ability to be nurses as formerly they were. And our children are generally now small and several of them have been sickly and weak most part of last winter. One girl in particular was ill near six months, who had been sorely afflicted with convulsion fits to such a degree as has made her incapable of walking but by use of crutches; and she had a fire in her chamber constantly for several weeks and one to sit up or to be with her in her chamber all the time, the fits being often upon her and suddenly taken.

In the year 1714 the committee gave leave by minute to hire a nurse into the house as occasion required. But upon enquiry found a nurse could not be had under 4s. per week & victuals and that if 5 or 6 of the family should be unwell at the same time a nurse would scarcely be willing to tend the sick in several places in the house, especially [p. 68] when they sit up all night. And if we have not suitable assistants who may be helpful from one place to another in the house as occasion requires, the sick & aged cannot have that due tendance they ought to have. These things, with how little work nurses do in the house and some of them wasteful withal, being considered made us very unwilling to take a nurse in the house. But in winter season it has been very hard for my wife and the servants, especially the servant maid who spent most of her time in that service and tending the children . . .

She has lately left this place alleging the hardness of her service here had impaired her health. She was a very good servant and would willingly have stayed with us, but could not go through the business. She used to mend the children's woollen clothes, which are generally but very ordinary and if they were put out to mend would cost more than they are worth and might make the monthly meetings very uneasy. She makes their beds and cleans their rooms, takes in and gives out their woollen and linen clothes, combs their heads, and dresses their sore hands and feet in the winter season, having many of them sores, which business alone takes several hours every day as may reasonably . . . be supposed where there are so many small children and 17 or 18 of them are girls, who are more trouble than boys. Which with the weak and aged and when sickness, lameness happens in the family we find pretty much uneasiness, the sick and weak complaining for want of tendance on the one hand and the servants, not being able to do the business, complain on the other hand, so that we find a real necessity for another maid servant, which my wife can better make appear to any of the committee who will please to inspect into the business of each servant . . . [than] I can demonstrate in writing. And it being expected my wife should see the provision &c orderly managed and seasonably distributed with frugality towards the house and a sufficiency towards the poor, and also to see the aged and weak have no just cause to complain for assistance, these particulars cannot be answered with ease to the family's satisfaction, to the helpless, and we who have the direction of the affairs under you, without the assistance herein mentioned.
May 1718.

73. [p. 69] Memorandum about brewing &c.

In the first place let all the brewing vessels be well cleaned & seasoned two or three days before brewing. Seasoning them is letting cold water stand in them two or three days.

Then fill the copper with water and light a fire under it 2 or 3 hours before the casks are begun to be washed (remembering to have them brought out of the cellar into the brewhouse in season, that no time may be lost while the fire is burning). Wash the casks once with cold water, hardly blood warm and twice more with hot water.

Before the casks are fully done let the upper back be well washed with hot liquor that it may be full by that time the casks & copper [are] washed.

Then let the mash tun and false bottom be washed, also the under back, coolers and the working tun.

By that time the vessels are cleaned, have a copper of clean liquor full up to the second curb.

Let the liquor, when whole, be put into the mash tun & stand there till the steam of it be mostly gone. Then put in all the malt and keep stirring it with the mashing staff. Then cover it close with a cloth and let it stand three hours upon the malt. Then let the wort be speedily let down into the under back; from thence pumped into the upper back.

Then, having a copper of liquor full to the first curb made as hot as thou can (if this liquor with second following copper liquor should boil it is not damaged) put it on the malt and let it stay on two hours, if more no harm.

Immediately after the second liquor is out of the copper put in the first wort to boil it two hours. Boil the hops according to the season of the year.

Then let it down into the under back and then pump it into the new upper cooler directly. And in summer let it stand or stay there till it is cold, but in winter let it be not quite cold.

Then let it into the little working tun and take half a part full and put to all the yeast, and when it hath worked and been beat down pretty well let half of it be put to the ale, the rest reserved for the small beer. Mind to beat the ale up well in the working and let it work in the tun till it becomes a little sharp in taste, then barrel it up.

[p. 70] After the second wort is drawn off the malt, boil it two hours and then convey it into the coolers. Let it be there till it's near cold. Then let it be put into the great working tun before it's too cold lest it should not work, and set it to working as soon as it's in the tun. So do a third and fourth mashing.

While the fourth wort is boiling let the upper back be full of liquor to be made hot to wash the vessels as before brewing.

Mind to pour three or four pails full of hot liquor down the leaden pipe lest it chill the beer before it comes to the barrel, and remember to stop it close after it has done working.

Let the cistern and long trough that carries the drink into the beer cellar be washed clean before the drink is tunned up and after it's tunned up.

74. Memorandum, 30 July 1718.

The monthly meetings seem . . . now inclinable to send friends into the house, such who are mostly aged and attended with such weakness as immediately want fire in their chambers and constant attendance therein, which is contrary to the direction of the quarterly meeting . . . If such as aforesaid be admitted (unless with due consideration) this may prove the consequence: either the house run to a very great charge for nurses (who heretofore were sent by the monthly meetings) or the poor, aged & sick want due attendance and also bring a bad report upon the house.

We suppose if an infirmary were made for the sick and weak friends one nurse would be able to attend 5 or 6 friends, having them together in one room, with more ease & better than 2 or 3 that are sick in separate rooms.

And if we had a sick ward and an order made by the committee that no nursing or separate diet should be allowed in the family, only to such as are removed into the sick ward, it may prevent craving disorderly persons who have resolutely kept their rooms contrary to the orders of the committee, also telling us they are not able to come down, neither [p. 71] eat the diet of the house, saying if we will not send up their victuals we may let them starve there, it will lay at our door, when at the same time it seems plain to us their stomachs were good and they were as able to come down as some that attended them. Some such persons as those we are seldom without, and if such were sensible they must leave their rooms and go into the sick ward, it might be a means to bring them willingly down to their victuals while able. We observe such as aforesaid loves to be by themselves, not being sociable in conversation.

75. A copy of Richard Richardson's letter to the . . . committee, not to be opened till after his decease. 17 December 1717, as followeth: Whereas in my last will and testament bearing even date with this writing I have given two of my houses in Thames Street to Richard Partridge and Richard Hutton, it is my intent the rents of them shall be paid to the committee of the workhouse for the use and benefit of the poor. Although in my will I say for Richard Partridge and Richard Hutton to dispose of as they shall see meet . . . it's my mind and intent that my daughter shall have her maintenance at the workhouse and table with the steward and his wife & such good accommodations as shall be meet during her life for the rent of the said two houses. But if my daughter's husband should refuse to let her live there, then it's my mind and intent that the committee of the workhouse shall, out of what they receive of the rents of my houses, pay into my daughter's own hands any sum not exceeding eight pounds per year towards her clothing.

In witness of all herein that it's my true intent and mind, I set my hand and affix my seal this 17 December 1717.

Richard Richardson

76. And further above.
[p. 72] The lease of all my houses in Thames Street is from the Dean and Canon of Windsor and pays £4 10s. the year and there is about 30 years to come . . . When there is but 6 or 7 to come it may be good time to renew, which I desire my executors or heirs to do without putting the committee to any charges . . .

77. The stow grate in William Townsend's room cost:
For 100 and 7 bricks at 2s. per hundred, 2s. 3d.
For six hods of mortar at 6d., 3s.
For one hod of coarse lime and hair, 8d.
For bricklayer's and labourers' work, 2s.
Per fine stuffs & working it, 4s.
Per one large iron stow grate, [blank]

78. A copy of a clause in Richard Richardson's will, 17 December 1717.
Item, I give and bequeath unto Richard Hutton and Richard Partridge all those my two messuages and tenements with their and every of their appurtenances situate and being in Thames Street, London, in several occupations of the Widow Steward and Thomas Hutchins, and all my right, title and interest in them or either of them for all the rest, residue and remainder of the several terms of years and time that at the time of my death shall be to come and unexpired, for them to dispose of as they shall think fit, freed and discharged of and from all ground rent that may be due or payable for the said two messuages. Which said ground rent: I order and appoint shall be paid out of the rents and profits of my four other messuages in Thames Street hereafter mentioned.

79. [p. 73: four lines of text from **74** have been copied in this place and then crossed out.]

80. [p. 74] Memorandum, 3 November 1718, at night.
Before William Townsend came to dwell here he was several times at the house and ate of the provision, heard the orders and the bill of fare read and expressed his satisfaction with them. Also consented to them before the committee. But not long after he was admitted he began to be uneasy, for there being an ancient man that lay very weak near William Townsend's room he said, to let friends assist one another in case of weakness &c is great cruelty, and the meetings ought to send attendance in or pay them of the family who do it.
Being once denied some ale for a particular and a sufficient reason he said, it was great cruelty in my wife in denying them it, although they have had ale more frequently than any of the ancient friends. And said, this house, which ought to be better than other charity houses, was worse in that the orders and bill of fare prevented them from giving away or selling their provision if they cannot eat it. And calls it cruelty to observe the bill of fare without exception, yet owns my wife is cautious therein and cannot allow a different diet to him because all the rest of the family will expect the same.
Being often abroad thinks it reasonable he should have the value of his allowance for that absent time in something more agreeable to his mind than the common allowance is, which is directly opposite to the orders and bill of fare and would occasion confusion and much contention about computing the value of such allowances.
He objects the beef is salt and the pork and mutton tough and not of a good kind and little of the provision of the house gives content. He

41

concluding, such provision is bought for cheapness and says, what need we be so saving in laying out others folks' money since we got nothing by it as we say.

He says, he never was a near man and if we do give him better than the rest they need not know it.

Note: we offer him a slice of cold beef, or any other meat when we have it instead of furmenty, milk pottage &c.

He often mentions his wife cannot eat the diet of the house and he sometimes, going to the cooks, desires his wife may have something prepared for her. Yet the ancient woman friend who lodgeth in the same room, also his maid, doth say, his wife is a quiet and contented woman, which appears the same to us and has a good appetite. [p. 75] My wife acquainted William Townsend that if his wife could not eat beef, pork &c she would provide several sorts of diet for her instead thereof, mentioning each particular sort of diet, which he willingly agreed to, but in a few days his mind altered alleging what my wife provided was of a cheap sort and was not good and did not answer his wife's time, and was uneasy. Then he said he would have the whole allowance of the house for himself, wife and maid, and he would provide what he thought fit, and accordingly they had it. And yet still uneasy, and told my wife that, since he had been here he had laid out 18d. or 2s. per week of his own money for other sorts of diet, which may very much tend to the lessening the good and plentiful provision of the house when reported abroad.

24 November. And being often abroad at dinner time as aforesaid and returning about 3 or 4 a clock and demanding his dinner and being reminded that the orders and bill of fare directs that absent persons must have no allowance, he will not understand the same with relation to himself which occasions many words, and at last he concludes saying he doth not believe the committee will be against their having their allowance, and selling or giving away or doing what they thought fit with their own allowance, saying, other charity houses allow the same, and has several times told us he will appear before the committee any time.

My wife acquainted me she went this day to give them a visit in their lodging room as she usually doth, he then, as he hath frequently done, began to contend about the provision, showing his uneasiness with one thing or another, and my wife told him she doth what lies in her power to make him easy and cuts him the best of any provision that comes under her hands and he tells her, he will not believe it . . . What to do further in this case we know not.

Now, it is our opinion from the best of our observation that what would make him easy is that he and his wife might have such diet provided for them as would suit their minds, without any [p. 76] regard to the orders or the bill of fare or what a general uneasiness it may cause amongst the rest of the poor friends of the family, several of them being worthy and thankful; neither considering the cost of such provision as would give content. He often objects against the cheapness of what we buy, though he knows not the price of it. And if the committee should adhere and give way to any discontented person or persons in this respect it would effectually set aside the management of the house as it's now settled by the orders and bill of fare. And what poor friends for the future may come to be maintained in this house may reasonably be supposed to expect the same accommodation, which will require more servants, which, with a different diet, will consequently much advance the expense of the house.

This being our present case and there seems to be a necessity the same should be deliberately considered and enquired into and things made easy on both sides, which cannot be unless the committee discourage any in the house who disregard their orders. Otherwise, the house may, if it hath not, suffer in its reputation and may sustain loss thereby. Also I and my wife disquieted and our reputation lessened in being thought unkind to the poor who are under our care, but a faithful discharge of our trust under you with regard to frugality toward the house, and condescension as much as can be allowed towards the poor.

Some of this affair hath been already mentioned to some of the committee, but finding the uneasiness not likely to cease inasmuch as all we can say leaves the friend as unsatisfied as the first, therefore we earnestly desire and entreat the committee would please do therein, as for the quiet family and well ordering the same, as they may see meet, that . . . a stop may in some measure be put to whispering, murmuring, backbiting and contentions which are directly opposite to us, my wife in particular, who undergoes the daily fatigue of it, and will be thankful to have a peaceable life not desiring to give any just occasion of uneasiness to the poorest friend in the house, but willing to assist them day or night as occasion requires and as hitherto she has done.

The foregoing as near as can be remembered are his own words & several insinuations, reflections & provocations are left out. Next morning paper in 86 page [**85**].

81. [p. 77] Memorandum, 3 November 1718, about William Townsend.
1st He ate of the provision, heard the orders and bill of fare, read & consented them when before the committee when admitted.
2d Said, to assist one another is great cruelty and meetings ought to send in attendance or pay them that do it (see article 2 of the orders).
3d Great cruelty to be denied ale (no mention of ale in the bill of fare).
4th This house is worse than other charity houses, because they may not dispose of their own allowances (see article 3 in the orders).
5th Cruelty to observe the bill of fare without exceptions, yet confesseth others would expect different diet also.
6th When abroad thinks it but reasonable to have allowance for that absent time in something else.
7th Objects the beef is salt, pork and mutton not of a good kind being bought for cheapness (friends who visit the house see the provision).
8th Saith, if he had better than the rest they need not know it (the bill of fare to be the rule).
He is offered a slice of cold meat instead of spoon meat.
He objects [to] his wife's [treatment], who seemed content (as informed).
Agreed his wife should have several sorts of diet, [with] which . . . he was

easy. Soon after refuses, saying, he lays out 18d. or 2s. per week of his own money.

[He] hurts the reputation of the house. He believes the committee would not be against selling or giving away their own provision (article 3). He is told the best of provision is cut for him in order to make him easy, he saith he will not believe it.

He first appeared before the committee 15 December 1718. Second time 12 January 1719 and then a minute made, page of the minute book 179.[1]

1. FSSWA, 'Best Minutes, 1714–1724', p. 179.

82. [p. 78] Memorandum, 20 December 1718.
This day William Townsend told me and my wife, he heard we had money out at interest and he did believe the reason of our being so pinching and sneaking was not only for the interest of the house, but in order that we might put something in our own pockets or advance our salary, and said, others in the family did believe the same, and would say so, as well as he. Upon which my wife desired to know if she did ever give him less than was allowed in the bill of fare and wherein she was so sneaking and pinching. After he had considered a little he answered, thou doth not set a candle on the stairs to light me when I come home at night, and I went one night into the old people's work room and there was no candle, and somebody asked my maid twice or thrice on that day we had pudding if I was at home. I believed thou would have been glad too, if I had been out that thou might have . . . a pound of pudding by me.

And thou made dumplings one day instead of figgy puddings. What did they cost? I suppose thou did it for cheapness, they were not worth above a farthing a piece. This is all he alleged for sneaking and pinching, which though not worth mentioning we are ready to render reasons for, as we this time did to him, but as appeared to us, to little effect.

Then we told him we did expect he should let us know the names of them friends in this family who told him they were of his belief concerning our being so sneaking and pinching and not only for the interest of the house, but that we might put something in our own pockets &c. We perceived he was very unwilling, but we insisted upon knowing their names, telling him such private reflections might ruin our reputation, but, if we were guilty let us now be manifested as such who are not fit for this trust. He said, ah, but thou art such an austere man and rules over the family with such rigour, like the Egyptian task master with clubs and staves and whips, that they dare not speak their minds, but I am not afraid of thee &c.

I desired he would explain himself how I was like an Egyptian task master. He answered, thou tasks the children every day as Pharoah did the children of Israel and rules over them with rods and whips and rigour just as the Egyptians did. Also said, a friend told me there was a boy abused in this house and died here, but we told him we never heard of any such thing, [p. 79] neither believed it, but if it had been so he had no reason to tell us of that there being no such thing in our time. But notwithstanding all these charges we still insisted to know the names as aforesaid. At last he told us, though unwillingly, it was Nathaniel

Puckridge and Eleanor Cobb (we admired at that, they having been innocent, contented friends and we had heard from several hands they had given a very good account of the house). But he said, he did suppose they would be afraid to own it they being ruled over with rigour as aforesaid. I told him I was resolved to try that and then desired him to go with me to Nathaniel Puckridge & Eleanor Cobb before the family. Neither was he willing to that, but said, that's the way for every body to know it. Yes, I said, the quarterly meeting shall know it rather than my reputation shall be ruined. And though he was unwilling to go, I was fully intended to hear it out. And accordingly we went in together, and first related the whole matter as aforesaid to Nathaniel Puckridge amongst the men friends. And Nathaniel Puckridge said, I admire at thee William Townsend, thou canst say any such thing of me. I never said or thought any such thing of them in my life, but have given a good account of the house [to] whoever enquired and thou knows I never said any such thing neither do I believe it. And said, I have heard thee say thou did believe they did not pinch so for the good of the house only, but believed some of it went into their own pockets. Then William replied, ah, I told thee they durst not speak the truth. Then I told them of the Egyptian rigour as aforementioned. The men showed a great dislike against such reflections and said they admired at William Townsend, saying, they never knew, spoke or imagined any such thing, & William had very little to say. Then we went into the women's room and spoke to Eleanor Cobb, and she said, I never thought or said any such thing in my life, and have heard William say that he did believe we were not so sneaking for the interest of the house only but to put something in their own pockets, and supposing he wanted to know my mind as he has at other times, I said, I did not know such a thing might be, but I did not believe any such thing. Also said, I admire at thee William Townsend thou has often times been drawing things from me but I hope to be aware of thee for the time to come. Then I spoke to the rest of the women friends about rigours and Egyptian slavery &c and desired them to be free and tell me now, before William Townsend, if ever they [p. 80] saw any such thing. Speaking quite the contrary, [they] expressed their satisfaction, saying they admired at William Townsend and did not think him to be such a man. He had little to say but as aforesaid: they dare not speak their minds, they are afraid of thee. Carry[ing] it off with a sort of a laugh, saying, now you have got a feast have you not.

A little before we came amongst the ancient friends William said, I once thought you were pretty honest people but now I have a sense upon me you are bad spirits.

This is part of what passed as near as I can remember leaving out several other reflections.

83. [p. 81. A page of undifferentiated accounts derived from the first volume of the house's general accounts and covering the period from 1702 to 1706: FSSWA, General Account Book, 1702–6.]

84. [p. 82] 16 January 1719.
This day William Townsend wanted a wafer to seal a letter and I told him I

had none but a sort of white wafer and I had not seen any such before then and told him he was welcome to them if he pleased. Then he desired to see them and accordingly I showed them. Then William held up his hands saying, well, this . . . is saving indeed, you are saving folks indeed. I never saw such saving in all my life, as is in this house. And after William had it over several times, then I told him, my sister gave them to me and I did not get them for savingness. Then I said, William, I believe if thou had been a little more saving thou would not have been blamed for it. Then William said, I have faith in my God that I shall never want. I said, I desire thou may never want. Then he said, ay, but you send us sprats instead of figgy pudding, you did it for cheapness and they were not worth above a penny. I told him, the committee was here and saw the sprats and thought them very good. He said, ah, the committee is thy cloak, they uphold thee, and began to clap his hands upon his breast and said, but there is consciences! consciences! consciences! and also said, the family complained because they had sprats. Said, there were no such thing, they loved sprats too well to complain, saying, they would rather have them oftener, but if any of the family do not love them we give them other victuals.

20 February. William said to my wife, what does thou make furmenty for us instead of rice milk for thou doth it for cheapness. She said, it was rather dearer. He said, how doth thou make that out? And after other discourse of that nature William said, you would not have had me come into the house at first. Then I told him, it was a pity he did come for he had done us no good nor himself neither. Then he said, it would do the house no good either. This was spoke at dinner time in the hearing of several of the family, also further said, the friends I was with last night would have me stay in the house, but I will not stay. I told him, if the friends did but know his behaviour, I did believe they would not be for his staying in this house. Then he said, aye, but the committee shall have the honour of turning me out.

[p. 83] 1719. His maid has been not well and has taken liberty to be very abusive, and we have often told her when she was well that if at any time she wanted ale or any other thing the house afforded, if she would let us know she should have it. And now she being unwell will not let us know what she would have, but saith, I do . . . not love to hear talk of things but to have them. Then her master said to my wife, what doth thou ask her what she'll have for that is but your cloak, make two or three good things and send them up and let her take which she likes of them. But thou sent a sick man a great dish of pottage stuffed with bread, was that fit for a sick man? But my wife told him, the man was not sick but had a very good appetite. Then William said, it's true, I do love good eating and drinking but I have been cruelly used since I came here and I shall not give the house a good word.

William frequently speaks slightingly of the provision to the children when they carry it up to him, and they have complained how he calls it pinching, saving &c. And when William perceives they are not easy with these reflections he has spoke harshly to them, saying, you are all alike & hold together.

I was informed William went to a friend's house and told him (before the servant maid that was not a friend), the allowance of the house and how they had sprats once a year when they were cheap about a penceworth each, but no other fish.

William Townsend went into the stable and the young man that looks after the children and brews &c asked William why he found fault with the beer, it being very good. William told him, he loved to find fault when he saw faults for he had been cruelly used since he came here. The young man asked him wherein he had been so cruelly used, and if he had not his allowance? Aye, William said, but I pay more than the rest. The young man said, but if thou should have a different diet from the rest it would breed contention in the family. Then William said, but if they had been prudent managers they might have given us different from the rest and none of them have known it.

7 March. William having given frequent reflections in the family as aforesaid, and my wife saw William go into the workroom amongst the children when at work and [p. 84] she was not easy therewith, and said, William, what makes thee come here? And [he said], he had liberty to go all over the house if he pleased and would come there for all her and stay as long as he pleased. She said, if thou had done good with going about in the family I should not have been against it but thou has done hurt. He said, in what have I done hurt? She said, in lessening us before the family and setting thyself up, and I do not intend to bear it as I have hitherto done, for if the commitee see but one half of thy behaviour to us I think it would make thee ashamed. He said, I will go before the committee at any time. I have been at war with you this twenty weeks, and the committee has had it in hand near this several or two months, and what have they made of it? But they shall have the honour of turning me out, and then began again to reflect upon the provision, only said, indeed the meat was pretty good, but told my wife she knew not how to manage it, and told her she ought to salt it and not just put it in nasty sour pickle to spoil it. Also said, I know what belongs to good house-keeping. But William did never charge my wife with spoiling the meat until now, but on the contrary has said, she was as fit for the business as any in London, only she was too sneaking and pinching &c. He also said, thou has been here seven years, and thou has learned thy trade. She said, yes, I hope to be here seven years longer in order to stand against such disorderly persons and think it will be as good a service as I can do for friends.

About this time William's maid missed her coal basket and she told my wife some of us had stole it. My wife said to William who then stood by, why doth thou suffer this maid to go on thus? He said, we have lost the basket. Then the maid answered again and said to my wife, thou are a cruel, bad woman, also said, pray God send us out of this house or else we shall be starved to death, and we had been starved before now had it not been for my master's pocket and my own, and she said, so would all the family if they did not buy victuals. And William's maid told one of our [p. 85] servant maids, [who] is not a friend, how she had told a great lie today and she was very sorry for it, saying, when she was out somebody asked her where she lived and she told them at the Quakers. But that was a great lie, for they were all devils or devil's people, and there was no Quakers in the house but in their room. And said, if thy mistress do not send up my victuals presently I will go out about five a clock and make such a rattle in the neighbourhood as shall make them all ashamed.

These are the consequences of having persons in the house who rule as masters in the family by having servants to themselves and doth not think herself accountable to any but her master, speaking unbecoming things about all things relating to the house or the government of it. Committee 9th [March] 1719, see page 184 and 187.[1]

16 April 1719. William Townsend said to my wife, thou doth not give our weight. I asked him in what I did not send him weight. He said, in meat, there wanted two ounces once and another time he thought 4 ounces, and another time 6 ounces. Then I said, William I can truly say I never gave thee less than thy weight nor any in the house I weigh to. Then he said, thou keeps bad weights then. I desired him to go down with me and take his brass weights and try my weights by his . . . (Note: he bought weights after [being] discharged the house on purpose to find something to expose &c.) Accordingly he did, and my pound weight was exact, and the half pound, his had rather the turn, but so little there was no room for William to take the least advantage in the weights. And the next day at noon I sent three pounds of pudding and William weighed it and said, it was two ounces too much, but, he said, it would help to make up the rest. And to the best of my knowledge it was as exactly weighed as any I ever sent him. Again at night I sent one of the maids up with William's butter and cheese and another of the maids went up with her unknown to me and came down and told me what William and his maid said to them which was as followeth:

The maid said, we have seen this half year how the poor has been cheated. I have heard of it four years ago but now I see it. It's a painted sepulchre, it's fair without but it's foul enough within, and it has been more craft than honesty or else they had not been here so long and this knavery will all come out. [p. 86] Then William said, they had never had their weight in anything but in pudding since they came, also said twice over, he could take his affirmation of it and it was base doings the poor should be put upon so. Then his maid said, aye, we may take our affirmation of it well enough, and a great deal more very bad of this sort.

Another time Hannah Newton went up and William's maid said, she would witness they had not their weight. And Hannah said, what signifies thy being a witness, thy master says thou art a liar, and if thou tells a lie in one thing thou will in another. Then William said, Hannah, I will tell thee, being a sober girl, we have made that up. And some time after that William's maid was railing as usual, and her master said to his maid, say no more now Mary till thou comes before the committee and it will have some service. Then the maid said, aye, but they are too cunning for that, they will not let me come before the committee.

1. FSSWA, 'Best Minutes, 1714–1724', pp. 184, 187.

85. (In the beginning belongs to 76 page [**80**]). William once began a discourse thus with me and said, thy wife is a near, sneaking, stingy woman, doth not thou know she is a near, sneaking, stingy woman. I said, no, I know she is not so. He still insisted I did. Then I was displeased at his insinuation and further said, I know her no more to be so than myself to be a robber. Yes, he said, she is a sneaking, stingy fool. I desired him to explain himself what he meant by the word fool. He said, she was such a fool as Christ spoke on in the gospel who built his barns bigger and scraped riches together and knew not who would enjoy it. Also said, we had but one child what need we be so near. I told him, what he called near on this account was no advantage to us only a just discharge of our trust. He said, he did not know that, could I say we got nothing by what we bought? I told him we did not directly or indirectly. But, to prevent such insinuations we desired of the committee that the friend Benjamin Mason might continue to see the provision bought, and accordingly he has seen it & also the receipts from one time to another. [p. 87] But afterwards I asked him what made him call my wife a fool and apply such an unapplicable or strange comparison to it. He answered & said, it was the sense that was then upon him. I told him, I thought it was a very dark sense. William also upbraided us and said, we got many a dinner by him, meaning when he dined abroad at friend's houses.

(Belongs to 76 page [**80**]). William told us there was others in the family complained of provision as well as he. I desired to know who, he said, Elinour [*sic*] Cobb. This friend lodged in the room with William's maid. Then I spoke to Elinour Cobb and asked her why she complained of her victuals to William Townsend and did not let me know. The said William Townsend frequently looked over her meat and asked her questions about it and once she said when she was eating her dinner he came again and asked and she told him, there was a little bit not very tender, but she would be careful of him in the future. Elinour pays for her own board, she has been very contented and given as good a character of the house as any I ever heard. But at other times before that time, William Townsend had told my wife he was not so well served with victuals as Elinour Cobb.

My wife bought a calves foot for his wife, and William cut it open and smelled at it and said, it was not sweet and it [was] bought for cheapness. And my wife told him, they should not have it if it was not sweet, and brought [it] to me and I advised her to show it to the women of the family & all agreed it was very fresh and good, and it was really good. And they will freely own, I mean the family, that what my wife buys for them is very good. And when William Townsend was told what the family said William's answer was, he would believe his nose before any in the family.

86. [p. 88] Having a poor craving man in the family who has been incident to complain and thereby get money of several friends who come to see him to pay what he had run in debt when his money was spent, and my wife went to see him one day and asked what money the friend gave him. He evaded it and was not willing to let her know, but at last owned one shilling. And William Townsend stood unknown, to hearken as appeared. About two weeks after, when my wife went to see them, William began to contend and asked her in a sort of commanding manner to tell him, what business she had to ask the poor man for his money.

Thou loves to get the poor folk's money from them. My wife told William, she did not ask him for his money. William said, thou will not tell me such a lie wilt thou. My wife said, no, I scorn to tell thee a lie, I only asked him and I had good reason for it. Oh, he said, thou loves to get the old people's money from them. I told him, I never kept one farthing of their money from them in my life. This and other reflections he gave at that time.

Another time a friend and his wife came to see the house who had a great respect for William Townsend and had been very respectful and loving to us. But when the friends came in it happened well I was then at home and soon did perceive the friends did not seem to me as at other times. But I took no notice, only seeing myself under some difficulty. But the friend went up with William into his room and stayed some time there. Then William carried them into the children's workroom to see them at work and to see the lodgings &c and I waited till the friends came down and desired they would please to see the provision. They seemed shy and dissatisfied. However I overpersuaded them so we showed the provision. And the friend's wife looked up at the cheese shelves [p. 89] and said, what is that, I think there is some Suffolk cheese. I told the friend, we had none of that sort since we came to the house, neither was there any before as we knew or ever heard of. Oh, said the friend's wife, but why do you not get them some pork, you have [had] pork but once since William came. Then my wife showed them the beef, pork, butter, cheese &c and brought the friends into the parlour and desired them to taste the house beer, ale, bread, butter and cheese. And putting a loaf that came first to hand, the friend's husband spoke low to William Townsend saying, this is special bread William, do you all eat of this sort. William said, again speaking very low, no, no, this is another sort of bread. I happened to be nearer William than he was aware of and heard him and so turned quick upon him and said, how, William, does thou say its another sort of bread, thou has had no other sort of us since thou came into this house, neither have we, save now and then a half quartern course loaf. William seemed hard of belief. Then I fetched several of the loaves and put them before the friends and it plainly appeared to be all of one sort of bread, and several friends was in the parlour at that time who admired at William Townsend, saying, they could not have believed had they not seen it. But the friends were all well satisfied at last and desired William to be content and easy. So the friends went away and very loving and we were glad of it. Also that we had opportunity to inform them.

87. [p. 90] The 7th day before William Townsend's coals were to be sent &c, Edward Carr went up with their coals and William Townsend's maid began as follows:

Saying, I do not care if I went out of this house this day if my master and mistress go with me that they may not be murdered as the rest has. The young man asked her who was murdered. She said, several or most had been murdered, and Elizabeth Stanton in particular, and said, when she was laid out she was as hot as that little cat. The man said, this is like the stuff thou used to say, thou called us all devils. She said, so you are, I can see little else except in our chamber. We have never had our weight or measure in any thing and if I go but into the yard I hear the old people say some of them has not their weight and some of them has good shares, but especially Elinour Cobb because she is with friend Claridge.

88. Lastly with some observations upon the whole &c.

William Townsend having dined at the house several times, and was very diligent in seeing the allowances cut both for the ancient friends and children and esteemed it very sufficient. Then I told William what exercise we sometimes had notwithstanding the allowances was so large, provision so good &c. William made answer and said we ought to have some in the family that might take part of the care from us. Also said it was very weighty and too much for us, referring to that passage relating to Jethro, Moses' father in law.

But soon afterwards when William could not prevail with me to turn the friend out of her room in order to give place to him without first acquainting the committee, he began to be very much displeased. [p. 91] So then William came before the committee, who did not comply with the aforesaid request though he afterwards acknowledged that he was better placed than if it had been granted him. But when William was admitted he owned before the committee how he was well satisfied both with the orders and bill of fare. Yet soon after he came into the house he began to insist on a different diet [from] the rest. Several times saying the rest of the family need not know it. And he was then of the mind the provision was very well for the poor of the family, yet concluded it was not reasonable that he and his family should be kept to the same diet, allowance &c. And about this time William began to have pretty much discourse with us and the tendency of it was (seeming in a very friendly manner) to prevail with us to go different from the orders and bill of fare relating to himself &c. And then I told him I was obliged to go according to the orders otherwise I should give a just occasion to the rest.

So then William began to try what rough treatment would do and especially to my wife, carrying himself towards her very unlike what might reasonably have been expected of him. But when none of this could gain what was then desired, his uneasiness soon took air in the family who was then in a quiet, contented frame generally speaking, so far as we could perceive. But William, in a great warmth of mind, made several undue reflections upon the orders and the cruelty of them, also on the bill of fare, and the meanness of the provision, and this was before his wife, the maid and the friend that lodged in their room, and soon after, the whole family came to know of their uneasiness.

So when I let the family know we went according to the orders and bill of fare and that hitherto we had done . . . [p. 92] the same to all, also told them we did believe none of them could deny the same. And said, I could not answer William's mind in doing otherwise now without partiality. And when the family understood that William endeavoured for something more than the rest, then they freely owned we did equally by them all, and said they had that which was good & enough of it and there was no cause of complaint, and it was well done of us to serve all alike. And they further said it was a pity William Townsend should have come into the family except he could have been content with what the house allowed as well as the rest.

Then when William Townsend appeared before the committee in order to answer to several reflections made on the orders and bill of fare which he both owned and stood by, though he got no encouragement from the committee, and yet after this William Townsend let in a strong belief that we were not so sneaking and pinching for the interest of the house only but in order to augment our own salary and put something in our own pockets. Saying, others in the family was of the same mind and would say so as well as he. But it proved quite the contrary when it was enquired into. Then William Townsend alleged it was the effect of fear in them, we being so cruel as he had told us just before. Also said, but I am not afraid of you. Now after William Townsend had tried several ways to lessen us in our reputations, which he could not bring to bear and his going out of the house being delayed, then he began to say the poor of the family was basely dealt by and has asserted the same to the servants several times. Also twice said he would take his affirmation that he had not his weight in anything except pudding since he came into the house.

And now we do clearly perceive that several in the family sides with him, having an eye to what William may do. They perceiving him very diligent in attending the committee when at the house, which may make it seem to them as if his case were otherwise than it really is or as if the committee . . . [p. 93] had not a sufficient power to deal with him as with others who have been disorderly in the family. They well knowing when any have been found in practices inconsistent with the peace and reputation of the house, such, if they could not be reclaimed, were speedily turned out, and did hope William Townsend would have been removed before this time, and the orders read in the family and some seasonable cautions given in order to put a stop to and expel the inconveniences that those disorders has brought in, before they had come to so great a head.

We do think that if the committee were sensible how hard it is for us, and my wife in particular, to reside constantly amongst a dissatisfied people some of which will give themselves liberty to say almost anything to serve a turn, you would, with us, conclude our post very uncomfortable, and therefore those things ought to be considered and if it appear we are unjust, as of late we have been rendered, then justice ought to be done upon us as such who are unfit for this trust. But & if [it] appear to the contrary, then we ought to have justice done us and none suffered to continue in this house who looks upon things with an evil eye, because their disorderly minds are not answered and therefore gives way to evil surmising and reporting things very wrong and that without a cause in order to injure the reputation of them who makes it their care to have things in good order to give content, that there may be no just cause of complaint. And [we] do hope it may be said we have hitherto served the committee faithfully both for the interest of the house, and the good accommodation of the poor to the best of our understandings and therefore we do with submission conclude it's reasonable to apply to and expect redress from this committee in our present grievances. And I know not one friend who have thoroughly known of our late treatment but who have thought it very unreasonable that we should be thus imposed upon.

89. [pp. 94–5. A short description of Hutton's method for balancing the house's accounts, produced in more detail above, **10.**]

90. [p. 96] Upon reading a proposal made to this court by John Bellers, Daniel Vandewall and Joseph Hackney, trustees for the corporation workhouse . . . [of] Clerkenwell in this county held by lease from Sir Thomas Rowe, Knight, granted in the year of our Lord one thousand six hundred and eighty five for a term of fifty one years, for ripping and new tiling the whole roof of the said house and for effectually making good all the rafters and carpenters work, and for new laying several floors and mending of others, and for altering the common sewer to prevent an intolerable nuisance that attends it, the performance of which work will upon a moderate . . . [computation] of workmen amount to above three hundred pounds exclusive of painting [&] plastering . . . [or] glazing; providing they may have an addition of thirty-four years added to the present lease, of which about seventeen years are yet to come. It is ordered by this court that it be, and it is hereby recommended and referred to John Milner, Narcissus Luttrell, Alexander Ward, John Offley, William Kingsford, John Ellis, John Shorey, John Law, John Tuller, Doyly Mitchell, John Metcalfe, and William Booth Esquires, twelve of his Majesty's justices of the peace of this county or any five of them, and such other justices of the peace of the said county as will think fit to be present, to take a view of the said workhouse and the other buildings adjoining held by the same lease at thirty pounds per anno. And the said referees are desired to inspect the repairs wanting to be done at the said house and see what in their judgement it will want effectually to make good the said repairs, also how much the said house and buildings will produce at the end of the said term, and to report to his Majesty's justices of the peace next general sessions of the peace to be held for this county, whether in their judgement it will be for the benefit of the said county to add an additional term to the said lease on the terms proposed, or to continue the said premises at the present rent for the remainder of the term of years now to come. And for that purpose the said referees are desired to meet at Hicks . . . [p. 97] Hall in St. John Street on Thursday come sevennight at ten of the clock in the forenoon, and to adjourn from thence to the said workhouse or elsewhere, as occasion shall require, and the cryer of the said court is to attend the said justices from time to time and give notice of their place and times of meeting.[1]
Per Cur. [Simon] Harcourt.

1. For the original of this document see GLRO, 'Middlesex Sessions: Orders of Court, vol. i, 1716–1721', f. 78. Also see FSSWA, 'Best Minutes, 1714–1724', pp. 185, 196, 199, 202, 204.

91. Pursuant to the order of reference above mentioned we whose names are under written do hereby certify that we have viewed and inspected the workhouse in the said order mentioned and the buildings thereto belonging and have received the proposal hereunto annexed which we do approve of, and are of opinion that it will be for the benefit of the said county to grant such a new lease on the terms therein mentioned in regard of the public use . . . [to] which it is applied and [of] the great charge and expense which will be necessary to be laid out to repair the roof and other parts of the said workhouse and buildings. All which we certify and submit to the judgement of the court, dated this 13th day of August anno domini 1718.[1].

John Milner, William Kingsford, Alexander Ward, John Metcalfe, John Shorey, John Venner, Doyly Mitchell, John Hayns, William Booth.

1. For the original of this document see GLRO, 'Middlesex Sessions: Orders of Court, vol. i, 1716–1724', f. 79.

92. [p. 98] To [his] Majesty's justices of the peace of the county of Middlesex appointed as a committee to view the corporation workhouse at Clerkenwell in the said county, held by lease at thirty pounds per annum granted to Sir Thomas Rowe, Knight, deceased, for the remainder of a term of fifty one years, and to inspect the repairs wanting to be done to the said house, and to see what it will want to make good the repairs and how much the said house and buildings thereto belonging will produce at the end of the said term and whether it will be for the benefit of the county to add an additional term on the terms proposed by John Bellers and others or to continue the premises at the present rent for the remainder of the present term of years now to come &c.

Pursuant to an order of sessions of the 9: day of July last: we whose names are subscribed, do on the behalf of our selves and the rest of the trustees, and persons entrusted and concerned in the said workhouse, propose that a new lease be granted to us or such other sufficient persons as shall be nominated by us from the trustees of this county for the term of ninety-nine years from Michaelmas next at the rent of thirty pounds per annum clear of all taxes and under the like covenants and agreements as in the present lease of the like premises.

That in consideration of such a new lease one hundred pounds shall be paid to the said justices and trustees for this county for the public use thereof as a fine or income upon sealing such a new lease. That in case the said workhouse shall at any time during the term of such new lease be converted or applied to any other use than it is now put to without the consent of the justices of the peace of this county in sessions, that then the leasees in such new lease to be granted shall either pay a further fine of one hundred pounds or surrender the said new lease and term so to be granted, save only that the present tenements (part of the said premises) as now divided and let out may be . . . [p. 99] continued as they are or converted into workhouses or otherwise as the said leasees shall think fit.[1]

Dated this 13th day of August anno domini 1719.

John Bellers, John Freame, Daniel Vandewall.

1. For the original document see GLRO, 'Middlesex Sessions: Orders of Court, vol. i, 1716–1724', f. 80.

93. [p. 100] Concerning spinning cotton &c.

1. Whether the smallness of the children doth not render them incapable of that care and exactness which is required in spinning cotton to advantage?

Note: the general opinion of friends who are tallow chandlers is that they are not capable.

If the committee should agree to make trial it is supposed that one person will be fully employed in instructing and managing the work for 10 or 12 children.

2. Whether the charge of wages and maintenance of such instructors would not exceed what can rationally be supposed . . . [will be] gained by it more than by spinning mop yarn?

3. If the profit of spinning cotton were much more than that of mop yarn why do not so many ingenious young women as now spin mop yarn rather spin cotton; interest leading them to carefulness without the charge of instructors?

4. Whether a woman can earn six shillings per week constantly the year long by spinning cotton, which we are informed industrious women at spinning mop yarn easily do?

5. Whether when spun it will as quickly return into cash as mop yarn, there being at this time as much promised as we can spin in a week, and have also several hundred weight more bespoke and to be delivered as soon as spun?

6. Whether it doth not require a larger trading stock than mop yarn?

7. Whether it requires rooms made warm with fires to work in, in winter time?

8. Whether, if after trial cotton should not answer to expectation, it would not be hard to regain the custom of so many who have at this time a dependence on our yarn and been brought to the house by some time and endeavours?

9. Whether it would not be leaving a certainty for an uncertainty by laying down our trade and taking up another we neither understand nor know where to procure customers for?

[p. 101] 10. Whether, if for want of trade &c, we should have large stocks of cotton in hand it would not sooner receive damage in colour or other ways than mop yarn, and if such damage should happen the loss must needs be more considerable of the one than the other, because of the vast difference in their value?

11. If friends (in good will to the house) should condescend to take our stock of cotton (or part thereof), whether in time it might not make the house as great a burden (especially if not done well) as it lately was in the case of mops, that is, when they lay at the monthly meetings till they were spoiled and good for little?

12. And inasmuch as we receive children into the house at about seven years of age, and can bring them to spin saleable mop yarn in about nine or ten days' time whereas we are informed that children of that age are not capable to spin cotton that [is] saleable.

If it should be objected that only the big boys should spin cotton and the lesser the mop yarn:

We answer, that the big ones are now employed in carding for and instructing the lesser, for we find by experience that carding requires more strength than the lesser children have. Likewise, when we take in children we are obliged to place them with the bigger for instruction so that if they were separated the work of the little children and new beginners (which generally are many) would in great measure be lost, the which would prove a small disadvantage to the house.

Now, we have found for want of that constant care and exactness which cannot be expected of so little children as ours are, that the yarn they now spin hath fallen short an halfpenny per pound of its value when done with care and discretion.

Therefore, what may be expected when they are employed in so difficult a work (with respect to mop yarn) as cotton is . . . may be well considered.

94. [p. 102] Observations on the spinning of worsted, or remarks on the proposals thereof.
1. Proposal: that wool shall be found by the employers provided sufficient allowance be made for the waste.
Observation: the employer finding wool, it appears there will be no gains to the house saving the bare earnings.
2. Proposal: that sufficient allowance shall be made for waste.
Observation: upon enquiry we hear that it will be considerable because the waste consists in the yarn not being drawn out fine to a certain length, as for example, a quantity of wool is given to be made into 12 skeins of yarn, and the children, for want of judgement, often bring in but 10 instead of 12, then 2 skeins is wasted and . . . according to contract must be made good in yarn value and paid for spinning only 10 skeins. And when the waste is allowed and the reeling paid for out of the same earnings (as the custom is) there will remain but little for spinning.
3. Proposal: that it's thought six weeks' time is enough to teach.
Observation: but we are informed otherwise. Yet admit it be enough, then after that time spent, the earnings are to be after the allowance for waste, reeling &c is deducted out of the wages which is sometimes 3d. sometimes 4d. and sometimes 5d. per day, more or less. And if it's intended the whole day or 10 hours, the working part of the day, then what time will the children have to learn reading, writing, arithmetic, play &c. We have done and now do order their work so that half the day, or the working part thereof, is allowed them for as before mentioned, besides the two meetings, one on the 3d and other on the 5th day, and [they] often have [the] afternoon to refresh themselves in the fields. But then, if half their time be allowed them in spinning worsted then consequently half the wages will drop, then it will be some $1\frac{1}{2}$d., some 2d. and $2\frac{1}{2}$d. more or less per day.
4. Proposal: that they shall be instructed at the charge of the house, the proposer to furnish proper persons to that employment.
Observation: with the employer and the instructor's wages (whether diet &c is [included] we do not know) it will [take] considerable charge [p. 103] out of so small and uncertain earnings. Now, in our present work one

man looks after all the children that spin and could do it if there were as many more and bring them to spin saleable mop yarn in three days time (without any loss by waste). The same man makes mops, brews and looks after all the horses & [is] ready on all occasions to be helpful about the house to the aged, weak &c. Note: we have found it very inconvenient to have our whole dependence of trade on one man. Whereas at present we are well furnished with variety of customers which have been brought to the house by time and some endeavours.

We have cast up what our children earn one with another and find it 3¼d. per day each. And the earnings and profit together for four years last past has amounted to about £567.

We cannot find that worsted will gain half the profit to the house as mop yarn when rightly considered.

At this juncture there is an extraordinary demand for worsted spinners, weavers' trade being good, but when the contrary they give less prices and [it is] hard to get spinning.

95. [p. 104] Of spinning worsted according to proposal.
1. Please to consider that by spinning of mop yarn we have got considerable profit on the yarn besides 2½d. per pound allowed for spinning, as also considerably by the sale of mops. Together near £5 per year (as we suppose), all which we shall wholly lose by spinning worsted, the manager providing work as by his proposal and we are only to be paid for spinning.
2. We find by experience one big boy and two little ones working together easily earn two shillings in ten hours, that is from six to six, allowing two hours for meal times, whereas it is not proposed they should earn above [blank] per day at worsted.
3. Spinning mop yarn requires but four candles for about 50 children, but it's thought worsted may require a candle to each wheel.
4. One man attends above 40 children and could attend 20 more, make mops, serves the horses, brews &c and it's supposed worsted would require one instructor to 10 or 12 children besides the manager.
5. Spinning worsted is paid for by the length and not by weight, therefore is the more improper for little children who . . . not consulting interest, are apt to follow that method which makes the most riddance of wool in the shortest time.
6. All the girls at certain times on particular occasions are obliged to leave their sewing &c and take to the wheel for a day or two, it may be in two weeks' time. And so much as they can spin mop yarn well we find it profitable, but if we should exchange mop yarn for worsted that profit would be lost. The girls' time for spinning not being sufficient [to] learn worsted to advantage.
7. We have found that for want of that constant care & exactness which cannot reasonably be expected from such small children as ours are (they being taken in at seven years of age) the yarn they now spin hath fallen short an half penny per pound of its value if done with care and discretion. Therefore, we cannot but expect a greater disadvantage by bad work [p.

105] when they are employed in worsted, the one so much exceeding the other in fineness.

8. We do conclude, if worsted were more advantageous than mop yarn, women who now spin mop yarn, and earn thereby (as we are informed) six shillings per week, would rather spin worsted, interest leading them to carefulness without charge of instructors.

9. Worsted being an oil wool therefore may require [more] charge in firing than mop yarn.

10. And it should be well considered if worsted should not answer to expectations, it may be difficult to retain the custom of so many who now have a dependence on our yarn and who have been brought to the house by time and some endeavours.

Note: spinning cotton was under consideration and some of our customers heard of it and if they should of worsted it might prove a disadvantage.

11. We have also found very inconvenient to have our dependence of trade on one man, whereas at present we are pretty well furnished with variety of customers.

12. Whether the proposer would be willing the children should have the best of the day for learning, that is from breakfast time to past 12 at noon and from two till five in the afternoon in the winter and the fore part of the day in the summer, which now they have. And if they should be deprived of that great privilege (the present income of the house affording the same without lessening the principal stock) whether it may not be a great discouragement to the house as likewise to the children, the chief end of spinning being only to inure them to an habit of industry by keeping them out of idleness, and not exert their endeavours to their utmost ability.

96. [p. 106] Spinning linen for sack considered, 25 March 1717.

We have cast up our children's earnings one with another and find it 3¼d. per day each, besides the profit by selling yarn and mops, whereas about half of the day is allowed them for schooling, play &c every day besides an allowance for meeting times on 3d and 5th days, and the whole gains on this account for 4 years last past is about £567.

When our whole dependence of trade was only on one man we were obliged to give long credit and have found it difficult to get the money at last. And the employer finding we had no other dependence has then begun to be uneasy and uncertain, also finding unexpected faults (the children being young and unlearned) as the work not being well, waste of goods &c. And if our children are employed in linen, which I am creditably informed their fingers cannot manage, there may be more demanded than the flax they work upon will produce. Then, if abatements should be required for such deficiencies, the profit to the house may prove very small considering the impossibility of any other advantage than the bare earnings, because the employer finds the work.

Unless the employer be a person [of] credit and great business our children who are now pretty many in number may possibly stand still for want of employ which would be an extraordinary inconveniency and . . . is too often the consequence when depending on one man. It would prevent their habit of industry, also prove a great loss to the house.

If the profit of spinning linen were more than spinning mop yarn would not so many of the ingenious young women who spin mop yarn rather then go to . . . spin linen, interest leading them to carefulness, not having occasion, like children, to be at the charge of instructors.

[p. 107] Whether a woman can earn six shillings per week at linen all the year round which we are informed industrious women at spinning mop yarn can easily do?

Whether it will require more fire places in winter?

Whether it may prove healthful for the children so young as are commonly sent into the house to be confined so much of their time at the linen wheel and the principal part of the rest of their time to sit at the writing school, and its reasonable to suppose but little time must be allowed for play if they make any reasonable earnings and have a suitable education.

Note: We have found it very difficult to manage the girls relating to their health since they have left the stirring exercise of the wheel.

We conclude it [is] much against the interest of the house to change the business in the summer.

By taking notice of new proposals we have been upbraided with uncertainty of depending on our yarn which may be the cause of discouraging the customers (especially if the report should spread) and make them leave the house. And if a new employ should not answer it might prove difficult to regain the custom of so many who now have a dependence on us and have been brought to the house by time and some endeavours.

We are informed that the friend who now makes this proposal was encouraged thereunto by an information that our present employ did not answer our expectations and our goods did not make a quick return and what the same seem more reasonable is, there being several poor people there always would willingly accept of some such business if any would please to employ them.

Richard Hutton

97. [p. 108] Memorandum, 18 October 1711.

The first night we came to settle this house there was an ancient friend sitting in one of the corners by the kitchen fire, and in the other, another friend who dined at our table and expressed himself in a very passionate way saying, do thou judge steward, if this be reasonable for him to sit in a corner when none ought to sit there, but I stand, I who are allowed such privileges by the committee . . . The two friends gave each other very unbecoming treatment.

The friend first settling in the corner alleged he had leave of the former stewardess to eat his victuals in the kitchen, also claimed the same privilege of us, which we dispensed with, though pretty many inconveniences attended it. Too many here to mention.

And the same friend being one day sitting by the fire in the corner, aforesaid, with his dinner on his knee, that being his usual way of dining, the other friend aforesaid came in and immediately seized the friend's chair hauling him & his dinner altogether into the middle of the kitchen, and then took a chair and sat down in the same corner himself. But the heart burning and contention that such work as this made in the family would scarcely be believed were it related, which consequently would not have happened had all been received on the same foot. For the several circumstances of inhabitants occasioned a striving who should govern, but too few were willing to be under government themselves and in this condition we found the family.

Some who have dined at our table have several times told us we were but their servants and maintained there to wait on them, and they paid more than the rest, saying, the house got by them but it got nothing by us. Also said, they had as proper a right to go into the pantry, and to be in the kitchen or parlour when they pleased as we had. And as for the provision, they told us it was none of ours and therefore they would have what they pleased and when they pleased. [p. 109] Now, when such treatment as aforesaid came to be known in the family the same expressions have been repeated by several of the poor maintained at the meetings' charge and frequently when the children have been present.

When my wife has been cutting out roast or boiled meat for the family at noon those who dined at our table would come with a large copper spoon like ladle and stand in her way, taking the gravy out of the great dish where the meat lay, thereby dropping upon and greasing her cloths, they not having patience to stay till we dined, when they might have gravy enough. And she has been cutting pudding into shares, if there was any place in the pudding that had more plums than the rest, they would cut out that piece for themselves. Those things and such like were bad examples in the family, especially when liberty was taken to do them when we was present.

And when my wife provided any diet for the weak or sick that was different from the diet of the house they would sit or stand looking on, asking questions. Saying that, the poor that was maintained at the common allowance had better provision and attendance than they. Saying, why might not they have such things, they paid more than the rest. And when prepared and set out of hand to cool, part of it would be eaten up unless some were placed in the kitchen to watch it.

And because we could not eat the meat quite so fresh as the rest of the family, they would be discontent and say we fed our table with little but salt meat on purpose that they might not eat much of it. And often told us that we grudged them victuals, though we frequently desired them to have a fresher sort of meat but they would not, but some times went from the table displeased and have told us we should hear of it on both sides of our ears. And we, knowing it was another sort of diet that they inclined to, have to keep our peace . . . otherwise they would have eaten nothing, [p. 110] though several sorts of diet for persons that are in health gives a just occasion of uneasiness to servants by hindering their business. Likewise, by such examples the rest of the family would find fault with the saltiness of the beef when it was quite the contrary. Insomuch as salt beef has been so commonly expressed that an ancient friend by way of complaint has said when eating, this beef is so very salt; when at the same time he was eating part of a fresh leg of mutton bought the day before.

And when we have had roast meat, some of our table would run their fingers into the meat while it was roasting and frequently handle the meat at table very indecently, which is offensive to decent, cleanly people; and yet when strangers dined with us they could behave themselves discreetly.

Also under a pretence of visiting and sitting with some of them who dined at our table has come in an intruding sort of people (on first days in the evening especially) who would place themselves in the kitchen and there sit smoking tobacco and keep our servants from the fire. And being told they might be of more service in their own families than to be here keeping our servants from the fire, then such have returned unhandsome language, implying as if they had as good toleration as we, saying, we could not hinder them, or words to that effect.

And when any friends have come to the house about business, I have been obliged to take them into the yard or some private room if the business required to be private, our parlour be so common and such and incidence being in them who claim privilege there, to hear and know all that passeth if possible and would take it amiss if they were desired to withdraw except it were some of the committee. And thus things have been reported amongst the family and thereby the affairs of the house made more common than was convenient.

These and many other difficulties I could mention which we have and do still lay under. And it seems to us very unlike it should be, otherwise, whilst persons are placed [p. 112: the number 111 was omitted in the original pagination] here on a different foot to the rest, who esteem themselves not only equal but superior to us, and we but as their servants, alleging the house gets by them as aforesaid.

So, for reasons already mentioned, we hope it may not be thought unreasonable if, with submission, we desire the little parlour and kitchen to ourselves. The former being fitted up out of the box with the committee's money on purpose for John Powell and his wife had he lived till they had been married . . . We have been told by one that dines at our table that in case John Powell had lived and brought his wife home, then they must not have enjoyed the privilege of the parlour as they now did, also said, but he was disappointed &c.

And when the committee was about placing us in this house they did propose that we should have some private instructions concerning the family and managing the affairs relating thereunto and when the friend brought the said instructions to us in writing also verbally expressed several difficulties that we might expect to meet with (which has proved true); likewise advised not to be discouraged thereat, saying we being young people it was hoped we might continue in the place until the house came to a better settlement. And likewise told us he had something to acquaint us with for our encouragement, which was that we should have the little parlour entire to ourselves as it was intended for the late steward and his wife as aforesaid. Only, he said, perhaps John Heywood might sit to keep us company some times. And some other privileges the friends also spoke of which was enjoyed by the former stewards and in course would come to us, but it proving otherwise therefore I omit mentioning them here.

And now the family is and like to continue pretty large, and [p. 113] various things happen relating to managing the affairs of it. And the parlour also the kitchen stands entire to do the business of the house, which makes our service more effectual, also affords us more satisfaction than if the committee should allow us one of the houses in the tenements for our accommodation.

And we do conclude that any who may or have placed persons in a public concern do allow such persons some suitable entertainment in this respect separate from them who are or may be under their care. For example, in the next house to us which is also a public concern, though quite of a different nature yet there is a suitable accommodation made for persons concerned as aforesaid. In the first place there is a good new house built for the captain or master, and is also a little house built for [the] poor woman that opens the gate and is entire to herself.

Now, for several reasons before mentioned and considering the trust committed to us, our care is or at least ought to be pretty great in such a family as this. We do therefore entreat the committee would with us see the necessity of our having a little place to ourselves and in order thereunto prevent for the future any friend or friends from being put upon us. We desire it not for ostentation, but as aforesaid, . . . that the business which requires privacy may be done accordingly, also to have a place to retire to as occasion requires.

I have lately been informed of several persons, and some of them are supposed to be pretty difficult, who incline to come into the house as boarders, and several are in the house now who are uneasy because they have not the like privileges. Therefore, if our small table were as large as could stand in the meeting room it may be questioned whether it could entertain all who might endeavour to be accommodated there, and yet those who have been gratified therewith and find our diet the same with the house, then [cause] uneasiness, contention and murmuring . . . to take place [p. 114] as aforesaid, saying, they pay more than the rest and have only the same provision. And if occasionally we have at our table a joint of fresh meat, though before we eat any of it, my wife cuts for the sick and weak in the family, and then if we only dine of it yet it will occasion whispering and murmuring in the family and we but conclude few in our place would be easy therewith.

But if the committee see meet to take any friends into the house in order to have a different entertainment we do conclude a large room with a fire place in it may be taken up on that occasion, also a new bill of fare made that differs from the common diet and if it proves to their satisfaction, then possibly we may go on more quietly than hitherto we have.

98. Proposals to &c.
We have found [it] inconvenient when friends have been sent into this house with expectations to be maintained upon a different foot to the rest, which very much tends to making them uneasy and laying waste the present bill of fare and orders of the house.

And if a different entertainment be thought necessary, we do conclude a large room must be fitted up for such friends to dine and be accommodated by themselves. Likewise a bill of fare made for them as may be thought sufficient and such . . . allowances to be paid as may answer the charge of a separate room, a fire by themselves, a different diet and servants to attend &c.

We are sensible, for several reasons (too large here to mention), it is very inconvenient that any who are maintained as pensioners &c should diet and be entertained in that small room allotted for the steward. Also, there being now a school and a school mistress, which formerly was not, and the steward &c finds it necessary for them to be accommodated with them in order to converse with them about matters relating to the family as time and opportunity permits.

[p. 115] N.B. Notwithstanding there may be different entertainment, yet for any to go contrary to the present orders of the house may prove very inconvenient as by experience has already appeared.

Richard Hutton

99. Our family have consisted generally speaking of a sort of dissatisfied persons very unfit for a community, also having amongst us as a people such who are very unskilful in their sentiments relating to the managing such an affair, also will very much resent it if their proposals and requests are not observed and that before them who may have a real sense of the matter as also sincerely desirous and industrious for the good of the house. Yet, when there is a dissatisfied family at home and many unskilful persons abroad, as aforesaid, who are more liable to hear reports than to give such bad reports a due consideration, therefore under those constant circumstances, [we] do conclude it very difficult and uneasy to them who under you has the care of such a family, also has and still may greatly tend to lessening of the house in its good accommodations.

Hitherto a remedy has not been found for those disadvantages that the house has all along and yet labours under, which, if it could, might produce those effects, viz: thankfulness and content in the family, the interest and reputation of the house, also quietness and composure of mind of the governors of it . . . I have had some thoughts on this matter as follows:

Which with submission is that you should have governors you may safely confide in, and the monthly meetings as well as the committee should be made sensible they are such as may be entrusted not in doing justly by the committee only but the family likewise, because doing right by the family has generally by some been the matter of question. Now here comes a passage into my mind may not be improper to mention though it's a little from the matter I am at.

[p. 116] Our new bill of fare was made in the year 1713 and doth considerably exceed the former bill of fare in quantity and so doth all parts of the provision in quality, except bread which was the same sort as now. I remember about that time the trade of the house was grown pretty much better than formerly it had been and soon after legacies frequently dropped in, so we began to get a little forward, which soon after took air and without doubt many honest friends were glad to hear it. But this did not please all, for so soon as our family heard of it I was told by some of them in a very untoward reflecting manner, saying, we heard the house begins now to save money by us every year and you ought not to get or save money by the poor. Also said that, friends gave not their money to the house with the intent but it was given in order to be laid out upon the poor in order to comfort them and not to be hoarded up. And in a small time after those . . . kinds of reflections were made abroad relating to the house saving money every year by pinching of the poor and over working of the children, and I have since been frequently told by the poor in the family that 3s. per week which their monthly meetings allowed for them was more than would maintain them abroad and therefore the house saved money by the poor. I mention these things by the way to show that notwithstanding the provisions are ever so good and the allowance plentiful, yet if our stock increase the poor do conclude that are not well used. Also observe, while here are reporters of stories abroad the house must be liable to be injured in its reputation.

Now to return to what I have thought might tend to remedying those things in a good degree if not quite, especially if it be well considered & rectified by the committee who well knows how to manage affairs of this or any other kind for the good of the house which of late in several cases has been done and has hitherto had good success for the encouragement.

[p. 117] When the monthly meetings as aforesaid do conclude they have such servants in this post, as may be considered in which do manage with as much prudence as they are capable, also with regard to justice in their trust in all respects, then the proper time may be for the monthly meetings unanimously to discourage such weak and unskilful persons as aforesaid, who by giving ear to reports do thereby give encouragement to the reporters of them, not considering how indirect it is for reports to be brought to them who are persons altogether unconcerned, when at the same time it's the care of each monthly meeting to choose suitable friends for their representatives in the committee (before whom all complaints may be laid, heard and if just, redressed) under whose care it is to visit the house every week to see that things are kept in good order and thereby are capable to give quarterly or monthly meetings an account thereof as occasion requires in [order] to maintain a good understanding between the said meetings and . . . the house.

Now, if the aforesaid meetings could be brought into a method and be hearty in discouraging such who incline to hear reports and by renewing general cautions in the . . . meetings from time to time to another when reports are heard, it may be a means to discourage the hearers. And as it comes to be generally known may put a stop to them who carry stories out of the house and do think it would make the family more settled, easy and thankful and consequently thrive better in body and mind.

And when the reputation of the house is thoroughly settled and carefully kept up from time to time, notwithstanding false reports or evil surmisings which hath hitherto been, yet it may be hoped that for the future the monthly meetings need not have so much labour and exercise in prevailing with their poor to accept of so plentiful a maintenance, but rather to advise and admonish them to be orderly in the house, endeavouring to walk worthy of so comfortable an accommodation which may fitly be compared to an estate which they cannot spend.

100. [p. 118] An estimate of the necessary repairs of the workhouse at Clerkenwell, viz:

Ripping and tiling the whole in the same form as it is now in, being 158 square at 15s. per square	£118 10s.
Materials and carpenter's work shoring and repairing the rafters and eaves boards	£30
	£148 10s.

101. This world's a city full of crooked streets.
Death is the market place where all men meets.
If life were merchandise which men could buy
Rich men would ever live and poor men die.

102. W.[illiam] L.[add]
Went away 8 October 1722. Boys gave the paper 16 November 1722, [which] is 5 weeks 4 days. Sent a letter to come again 26 November 1722, 7 weeks. Appeared to answer 12 December 1722, [which] is 9 weeks 2 days. Brought a paper owning the fact, 7 January 1723, 13 weeks.

Was then ordered by the committee to prepare a paper against the next committee in order to give the steward satisfaction for his revilings and false charges which he could not make out. But William Ladd went into the country and it was 2 months before he came again . . . The committee met at the house 4 March 1723, 17 weeks, then William Ladd appeared, but instead of giving satisfaction he said, he came to demand satisfaction, and his appearance and behaviour gave so great an offence to the committee they recorded it and advised me to take no satisfaction at all, esteeming by his appearance not worth notice, concluding that he wanted to be from under the censure in order to preach or deceive some persons &c and then told him it would be best for him to be gone over sea.

103. [p. 119] An estimate of the intended alterations and necessary repairs in the aforesaid work-house.
Imprimis:

To raise a storey 8 foot high and battlements front and rear of brick which contains 6½ rods at £5 10s. per rod	£35 15s.
Seven beams and ceiling joists containing 31 square at 3s. 4d. per square	£52 14s. [*sic*]
Roofing 37½ square at 30s. per square including the guttering and eaves boards	£56 5s.
Plumber's work 60 plates of lead for 7 gutters at 14s. per plate	£42
To a column in the meeting and 7 posts under the gutter plates	£3
Pantiling 30 squares at 20s. per square	£30

Twelve sash frames and sashes with English glass, weights, lines & pullies		£25 10s.
Plasterer's work, 450 yards of lathe & plastering at 9d. per yard		£16 17s. 6d.
150 yards of rendering at 3d. per yard		£1 17s. 6d.
600 of stopping and whitewashing at 1½d. per yard		£3 15s.
Ripping and tiling the two sides &c.		£82 15s.
Carpenter's work and materials		£20
		£370 17s.
. . . Deductions of allowance for timber in the old roof	£30	
For the old pantiles	£14	
The difference between sashes and common windows	£13 13s.	£57 13s.
		£313 4s.

104. [p. 120] Sundry disorders, 30 March 1720.

It would be tedious, also unpleasant, to hear the whole of the provocations rehearsed; also here are too many to mention the particulars of those who in their turns are addicted thereunto. But, the ground of it all is their being under any obligation, either with respect to the orders of the house, bill of fare and the diet as therein mentioned.

And when we have the advantage of very honest servants, who, equal and just in their places and not willing to comply with some in the family in answering requests that are not reasonable nor according to the orders and bill of fare, also contrary to our knowledge, then such servants are liable to be misrepresented, also frequently insinuating against them to us & notwithstanding we know such complaints &c to be without any cause. Therefore cannot take such notice of complaints as aforesaid as they may expect. Then what follows from them is that we hold with and incense the servants against them, when on the contrary it's very well known our frequent practice hath been and still is to give the cook-maid a thorough understanding of the orders and bill of fare, the allowances &c, also do advise and desire her and the rest to give no just occasion to any but to give each their just allowance, especially such who have an appetite to dispense therewith.

And being willing to gratify any in the family who desire spoon victuals for breakfast &c, instead of their allowance in butter and cheese, then we make them water gruel, put butter and sugar in it and when we have rice milk, furmenty we give them that, and then they will take up beer perhaps drink a little of it and set the rest aside in their pots, so that great waste has been made by taking up more beer than is drunk, in throwing it away, or giving it to the children unknown to us, which has been very inconvenient for them, also putting it at other times into the children's mugs, where it has been spoiled, and then laying the blame upon the children, saying, they left it there, notwithstanding we are certain they either drink their beer or return it . . . If we prevent their taking beer as aforesaid, which my wife on the 1st instant did, and was treated by Henery West in particular as follows:

[p. 121] 30 March 1720. Henery West said to my wife, what, will thou take my beer. Then she told him, he had water gruel with butter and sugar in it. Also told him, she thought he had no occasion for beer in the morning except he took out his allowance in butter and cheese as the rest did. And she further said, thou sees I have taken John Knoll's beer likewise. Then Henery said, oh, thou only took his beer for an excuse because thou would take mine, and it's barbarous & cruel indeed of thee to take the beer away, and more of this sort. Also said, I came home last night at seven a clock and the maid would give me no supper, but all the city shall know it. My wife said, if thou tells the whole town it was nothing to her. Also said, she did nothing to him but what was just & according to order. Then Henery said that, indeed here is a great deal of justice but here is no mercy, and I have been very barbarously and cruelly used since I came here, and said, Quakers! And one that stood near him . . . [said] over again, Quakers! . . .

But Henery West will not allow us liberty to speak about the orders and the bill of fare, but he will be very abusive and give us very undue treatment, calling us lying, envious creatures, proud, arrogant, barbarous, cruel &c, saying, we made them orders on purpose for him, and them that put him here would have had him better entertained here and we hindered him, and he valued us not, but will go before our committee with us at any time, and that very instant spread abroad his hands and declared himself an innocent, peaceable man, also in very rash manner calls aloud upon the name of God to witness for him and against us, likewise calling upon the family to witness the same.

Now we desire it may be considered how liable we are to be abused and misrepresented abroad when without any occasion it is so frequently done at home in the hearing of the ancient people, servants and children, also how difficult it may be to have common justice from people who give themselves such liberty, and then immediately to vindicate their own innocence, and account themselves altogether the injured persons. It seems not only difficult to us as aforesaid, but almost impossible to have right done us, and such . . . [p. 122] persons brought into good order.

And as their violent and fierce accusations, and several of them secretly holding together therein, also denying their abusing of us as soon as it is done, seems plain to us by their threatening it's intended to awe us, or bring us in fear, as if we could not be capable to make our complaint appear just against so many who . . . are so resolute in what they assert or deny as aforesaid.

And if the family goes on as they have for some time past we shall be liable both ourselves and the rest of the servants to be abused as aforesaid and obliged to give up more of time than other business will allow, in order to clear ourselves of so frequent insinuations, for the family having nothing to employ themselves constantly with, most of their time is spent in going . . . abroad, and pretty much of their conversation at home consists in strife and contention, the women especially. And at other times when they are a little more easy amongst themselves, then are they incident to whisper and contrive together against the house and those who have care thereof.

The orders have been read once by the committee to the ancient people since they are altered, and the little regard that appeared to them by several, though seemed quite otherwise before you, has discouraged me from reading the orders since to them though [I] frequently remind them what are therein contained. A passage relating to this is in pages 126 & 127 [**106**].

105. [p. 123] The school master's observations on the family was taken at the same time, which is as follows:

School master's observations &c, 30 March 1720.

People who are brought into adversity by their own mistaken conduct, either in the management of their affairs or living above their abilities, are for the most part pretty much cast down, and whilst under this state of constrained humility seem very willing to comply in promise with a more regular and orderly way of living, though never so repugnant to their former practice, on condition their indigence be supplied. But as soon as plenty is enjoyed and that taken away which caused such an alteration of mind, their former ill humours & disposition, that was not taken away or changed, but only confined and depressed, begins again to manifest and discover themselves [in] contention against order.

The truth of this too evidently appears among the ancient people in this house, for several of them being at their coming in under the aforesaid circumstances, viz: in want, in which condition, when . . . the orders and bill of fare are read, condescend enough in promise with whatsoever is therein contained. But these resolutions hold not long, for when they once come to sufficiency the want whereof produced the aforesaid condescension, they then forget their former condition and neglect the performance of the promise . . . Their natural dispositions begin unseemly to manifest themselves in opposition to good order and with disturbance to those that are concerned to contend for it. They, indeed very openly, and that too frequently, declare a dissatisfaction with the victuals in very railing and unsavoury expressions, even in the presence of the children, servants &c. And because they [are] living in plenty their desires begin to wander and their humours crave for such things as are not according to the bill of fare, nor could be prepared without a considerable addition of servants. For who can suit everyone's humours in respect of diet, unless each at every meal have according to their own appointment. And commonly when such are sent them contrary to their desire though according to the bill of fare they fail not to show . . . [p. 124] their dissatisfaction therewith, either at home or abroad; at home in sending it back or else in contending with those that bring it or by some such like unseemly deportment at the reception thereof, or else shortly after will signify it one to another abroad by telling false reports to those whom they imagine may possibly adhere and so endeavour to bring a public scandal upon the house.

Now as [to] their behaviour and carriage, one towards another, it is often as it ought not to be, for many times there is contention, ill evils and disrespect showed and are unwilling to help and assist one another in weakness.

Thus having given a brief hint of things partly as they are, it comes now in course to consider of their consequence (which seems chiefly to relate to three particulars) and also of the improbability of their amendment.

1st To the governors of steward and stewardess, who are first and chiefly and most frequently concerned against such appearances and so liable to undergo the greatest exercise, for who can maintain their post meeting with resistance without cause of disquiet and uneasiness when one discharges their duty and trust faithfully and administers in their office justly, and yet meet with little but displeasure, finding fault, discontent & uneasiness from those they administer to, must certainly have but small encouragement to persevere nor much comfort in their places.

2d To the children, for the effect thereof we are sensible of an ill consequence to them when they see ancient people (whom they are incident to take for example especially in such matters) find fault, murmur and dissatisfied with their victuals &c. What may they most reasonably think and incline to? Surely this disorder which so obviously appears in ancient people will raise no good dispositions nor inclinations in children nor beget any respect in them towards their governors nor values and good thoughts of the place, neither content with the fare nor gratitude toward those that maintain them.

3d And children thus vitiated, ill affected & prejudiced [p. 125] by precedents have as often as they see their relations the advantage of being further injurious, for they will readily tell whatsoever they see transacted and likewise their own sentiments of things and promulgate false reports, so become very active to discourage others.

To the house such must needs be of very bad consequence, for when those that so liberally participate of such benevolence and large extent of charity convey (instead of gratitude) false and scandalous reports concerning the administration & management thereof amongst those that are benefactors or any way concerned in contribution to the same, will undoubtedly very much diminish friends' satisfaction they might justly expect in the dispense and bestowing of their charity and tend to discourage and prevent others that might be disposed for the advance of the house.

Now the amendment of these things seems very improbable whilst the house remains under the same circumstances. If the committee should bring them in question about these doings they would directly deny them, for I [have] both heard and seen some find fault with the victuals in a very contemptible way & shortly after of his own accord utterly denied it, saying, there was no better victuals in the kingdom, or in words to that purpose. Or if they should use some sharpness to those most addicted to disorder, by displacing them they would account themselves to those that probably believe them misrepresented and severely dealt by. So would they more vigorously endeavour to publish the above named reports, and those left behind would not be heartily reformed, but only under a little awe and fear, for its a very difficult task to produce order where the contrary is implanted and sprung up. And most know that it's no easy matter to bring aged people, that love nothing worse than to be under government, from their accustomed habits.

Josiah Forster, School master.

106. [p. 126] 30 March 1720
This committee having been diverse times and from sundry persons informed of several persons in this family who have been and it's to be feared still are very disorderly and refractory therein, likewise we ourselves have now as at other times seen the undue liberty some in this house have taken:
1. In contempt of the provision which we know to be very good and well ordered and not inferior to [that] which many worthy honest friends are thankful for, who work hard for their families and are contributors in order to maintain you here; and all that is desired for the charge and labour bestowed is that you be helpful to each other & thankful which is the truest of holiness, but its our present exercise to see the contrary so much appear.
2. In condemning and lightly esteeming the good and reasonable orders of the house without which such a family as this cannot long subsist, and we do conclude such who treat the orders as aforesaid will not cheerfully comply with the same according to their promise before the committee when admitted, otherwise could not have been taken into this house.
3. In the frequent and undue treatment (and that before the servants and children) which is given to the steward, and stewardess who . . . the committee has placed here and are satisfied with them as suitable persons to govern and be entrusted with the affairs relating to this family. And we do hereby give you to understand that they shall not be imposed upon for the future as hitherto they have been.
4. In frequent going abroad spending much of your time out of the house contrary to the aforesaid orders, and thereby having opportunity to murmur and complain, likewise carry false reports against the house (also those who have the care thereof) to such persons who are not well disposed towards the said house, and thereby are liable to be imposed upon in hearing bad reports which several of us have heard of abroad. And if we hear reports of this nature . . . [p. 127] for the future [we] may think it necessary to find some constant employ suitable for the ancient people as well now as formerly which may tend to the reputation of the house, also be an advantage to such persons in preventing them for the future from such idle wandering habits in carrying stories & whereby they injure themselves and likewise the house.
In the year 1720.
This relates to a passage in pages 120, 121 & 122&c [**104**].

107. [p. 128] Dear friends,
These are to acquaint you that we are inclinable to part with our present school mistress, also desire your assistance in recommending &c some suitable person to us in order to supply her place, if you incline that the sewing school may be continued for the future, there being but few girls in the house.

We have not hitherto much disputed the charge and considerable loss the sewing school has been to the house (for near 5 years) in taking up the whole of the girls' time, which they have worked for so small earnings. Yet with you we esteem it necessary that they should have some education of this nature, though we conclude it has not yet so fully as could be desired answered the good intent therein proposed by you, to wit, a more thorough qualification for good servants.

The girls come into the house about the eighth year of their age, commonly stay until about 13 or 14 years old, and part of that time is spent in learning to read, write & cypher. And as to the sewing work, it has generally been sent in pretty fine, therefore the children are scarcely brought to finish any work. And notwithstanding that, when any friends that are good housekeepers would take a girl out in order to bring up to housewifery, then several of their parents, mothers especially, have not been easy therewith, esteeming their children qualified for better business (as shop maids, seamstry &c) by reason of the education, and also has been incident to influence their children not to comply willingly therewith.

And we are of opinion that if the sewing work were not of the finest sort, but such sent in as the children might in a reasonable time learn to begin and end their work, it might the better qualify the girls for your aforesaid intention.

Also if the girls do not spend so much of their time at the sewing school it might possibly prevent their parents from so much disesteeming the station of household servant, though in good families; for now it is too common amongst our young women who are servants who cannot much use their needle, to learn any business whereby they may live at their own hands, though [this] often proves to their disadvantage in diverse respects. And we do suppose you may have experienced that . . . [p. 129] when young women come out of the country who may have had but little education of this nature, yet have been very good servants and not so incident to be unsettled in their places as some who are more instructed in learning as aforesaid. We mention not these things to prevent the girls from having a suitable education in order to qualify them for good servants, but rather friends, that both you and we may in a friendly manner consult together in this weighty affair in order they . . . may not only be qualified for good servants but also tenderly be made sensible how reasonable it is for them to comply therewith in serving friends who have had a tender care over them.

And we are obliged to let you understand we are now very sensible that unless a very conscientious person be placed here for a school mistress who may be free from perplexing circumstances, also exemplary and diligent in order that a good behaviour and an industrious disposition may be early . . . cultivated into our children, otherwise the good intention proposed by you and us may not be answered.

108. Some reasons.

Our house is a house of charity for aged, sick, lame, blind &c, also for poor children whose parents are not in ability to maintain them, and some who are fatherless and motherless children and would come to the parish if we did not take care of them. And in-as-much as we do not only maintain those but also the rest of our poor at our own charge, also pay proportionally towards maintaining the parish poor, therefore we esteem ourselves aggrieved by taxing the same house &c so high and do conclude the like is scarce known to be done by any houses of this nature.

Objection: but it is not a house of charity according to law.

Answer: we are informed it is lawful for us or any protestant dissenters to set up houses of industry in order to educate their children therein. And inasmuch as we maintain our own poor and pay our equal proportion of the poor's rates. Through mistake carried to 132. [p. 132: pages 130–1 contain the house's general accounts for 1721.] Also then with submission we do conclude it to be consistent with justice &c in doing as we would be done unto, by allowing the like privilege and indulgence to a work of so general a benefit as the education of children in sobriety and an habit of industry.

Objection: but you make your children earn their livings.

Answer: because we have not been incident to complain of our charges, therefore strange things have and still may be supposed. But several of our children are very small and scarcely earn an half penny per day, and them that are bigger spend pretty much of their time every day in learning reading, writing &c which, with the time allowed them for play, makes smaller earnings than may be supposed; and the principal advantage proposed by that little work the children do is in order to inure them in an habit of industry and they are well provided for respecting victuals, clothes &c. We also keep a school master, likewise a school mistress to teach the girls sewing, therefore it may be reasonably thought or however, easily made appear, that there is a great disproportion between the children's earnings and the charge that maintains them.

109. [pp. 133–5. The house's general accounts for 1722.]

110. [p. 136] A copy of a paper &c taken to Richard Hutton, steward of friends' workhouse.

15 January 1723.

Loving friend, Thou art desired to acquaint John Albury that his misbehaviour in friends' workhouse has been considered by us and that unless we hear of a speedy amendment we shall be obliged to complain to the committee in order that he may be turned out of the house. Also thou mayst let the said John Albury understand that after he is turned out of the house for his disorderly conduct therein . . . it is probable that friends will think themselves entirely clear of him and if so, he may not expect any relief from the monthly meeting for the future, notwithstanding necessity and distress he may bring upon himself by his wilful, inconsiderate and disorderly behaviour as aforesaid. And for caution thou art desired to read this to him which he would do well to consider before it be too late.

Gilbert Molleson, George Wingfield, Richard Saunders, Phillip Storrey, Richard Hutcheson, Nathaniel Beard, John Russell.

111. Laid out for John Wilson when sick, weak &c.

6 December 1718	Quarter pound chocolate		10½d.
12	Physic		3d.
16	Anastringent juleps		10d.
29 January 1718 [1719]	Quarter pound chocolate		10½d.
5 February	Two pounds of sugar	1s.	
9	Quarter pound chocolate		10½d.
	Cinnamon		4d.
16	One pint of claret, 9d.; quarter pound sugar, 3d.	1s.	
25	Quarter pound chocolate		10½d.
19 March	Half a pint of claret, 4½d.; half a pound of double refined sugar, 6d.; half an ounce cinnamon, 4d.; and 4 ounces burnt hart's horn		6½d.
20	Oysters		2d.
23	Quarter pound of chocolate		10½d.
26	Oysters		3d.
	Conserve of roses as by receipt book, with juleps	5s.	
6 April	Cheese cake		1d.
7	Oysters		2d.
10	Fish		2d.
18	Oysters		3d.
5 May	Conserve of roses at sundry times	2s.	6d.
12	Half a pint of wine, 4½d.; double refined sugar, 6d.; and 4 ounces of burnt hart's horn	1s.	2½d.
22	Half pint claret, 4½d.; quarter pound bisquits		7d.
	Cheese cakes		1d.
26	A pint of claret		9d.
28	Quarter pound chocolate, 10½d.; bisquits 1d.		11½d.
7 June	Pint and a half claret	1s.	1½d.
9	Half a pound six penny sugar		3d.
15	Pint and half of claret	1s.	1½d.
17	Half a pound of double refined sugar		6d.
	Fish		1½d.
20	Quarter pound chocolate		10½d.
23	Cheese cake		1d.
25	Quarter pound bisquits, 2½d.; and cheese cake, 1d.		3½d.
		£1 5s.	10½d.

112. [p. 138] Conserve of roses before mentioned was taken morning and evening in red cow's milk. He had chocolate to breakfast, and having new laid eggs in the house he had them poached &c, milk thickened with flour or eggs, also bread pudding.

113. William Brady's accommodation

I was desired to inform any friends or others concerning the accommodation William Brady had while in this house, because several strange reports have been spread about as if he was starved while he was here. He was in the house betwixt two and three years, and did signify here that he seldom has his health at home. And here also he was very often not well, but especially in winter, when he was mostly incapable of either learning or working. Also seemed to have a natural aversion against both, together with a very uneasy disposition which was supposed to hinder the child from thriving, also increase his distemper, which was concluded to be a consumption; likewise very incident and intermitting, . . . also a looseness, and therefore the doctor advised that he should have his own country air.

He did no business (except a few days at school) from 30 November 1722 to 2 September 1723 which was until the time he went out of the house. And all the said time was accommodated in the kitchen. And for his diet, when it was thought convenient for him to eat meat, he had then mutton, veal and pork, being a great lover of the two last, and was esteemed very suitable for him. And sometimes he would desire roast beef which he also very much liked and had it accordingly. And concerning the quantity of meat, he was not kept to any allowance but had it cut till he said he had enough. In the third month of the two aforesaid years . . . he had red cow's milk and conserve of roses the first thing in the morning and had the same again about the fourth hour in the afternoon. His breakfast, . . . pretty often in the winter time (or when he had his looseness) was generally half a pint of chocolate with 4 ounces of bread toasted and sometimes rice milk, milk pottage or mutton broth. And having new laid eggs in the house . . . he had them sometimes poached. And when meat was thought improper for him [p. 139] also he had milk thickened with eggs or flour. Likewise he had bread pudding, fresh fish or anything in reason was got that the child inclined to eat.

He had diverse times papers of bezoar powders when the fever was upon him, also juleps and cordials when the looseness was upon him and then his common drink was made of powder of hart's horn, cinnamon and double refined sugar, and after his supper, the last thing when he went to bed, he had a bit of bread toasted with a coffee dish of claret burnt with cinnamon and double refined sugar . . . And it is not this child only, but any in the family either old or young are accommodated in the like manner or as their distempers, weaknesses &c, requires. What is herein related is really matter of fact and several are now in the house that was eye witness and can testify the truth of what is herein related, notwithstanding what may have been unfairly drawn from the child.

It hath sometimes happened that the children have been put here by their parents whose former circumstances has been pretty good, and has seemed as if their minds were somewhat above the good and reasonable orders of the house, without which such a family as this cannot long subsist. And therefore are incident to request things that cannot be admitted or without setting ill precedents, breach of orders &c. Then such friends have been liable to sow dissatisfaction and disrespect and that even before their children who ought rather to have a good esteem implanted in their minds for them who have the care over them and their education &c. But instead of advising their children as aforesaid, such parents have been very incident in a surmising, doubtful mind to ask their children many questions (about their work, victuals, correction &c) and the children can quickly discover their . . . parents' dissatisfaction, esteeming it then a proper time to gain a point to themselves having so fair an opportunity given. And we have observed that children have taken liberty to report things altogether not true and that might never have been thought on by them if they had not been led to it by the unskilfulness of their parents.

And inasmuch as it is mostly against the natural inclination of [p. 140] children (especially who have had much liberty) to love any less liberty than they have been accustomed unto, and again, liberty, change and new things are very agreeable to children, and therefore may reasonably be concluded they may be liable to say diverse things not true in order to gain what is so agreeable to them, especially when they find how easily they can have an influence upon their parents as aforesaid. And things of this nature have been a great hurt to the poor children who otherwise might have been very easy and well content. Also has brought trouble and exercise upon those who have the care of the children and which as likewise, very undue, tends to the lessening of the good and plentiful accommodation of the house.

And inasmuch as diverse bad reports have been spread about relating to this child's accommodation as aforesaid, it was esteemed reasonable a true state of the case should be sent, which I have done accordingly and conclude your respectful friend.
Workhouse, 29 July 1724.   Richard Hutton, Steward

114. Esteemed friend John Tanner,
    It was thought convenient that something of this nature should be sent inasmuch as divers false reports have been spread about relating to William Brady. Therefore, [I] desire thou wouldst please to desire friends that the enclosed may be read in your monthly meeting in order for their information concerning the accommodation &c of the house. So with mine and my wife, kind love to thy self &c, I remain thy obliged friend,
Richard Hutton
Workhouse, 29 July 1724.

115. [p. 141] Memorandum, 18 July 1726.
    It very much [harms] us in the managing affairs in the family when the children's parents treat us not only with disrespect but also abusively and that in the presence of the children, servants &c; especially when they say they have authority for what they do or say which makes the children very

insolent, subtle & stubborn, frequently contriving to spread false reports. And we do suppose that the children was scarce ever in general corrupted in respect to speaking untruths, idleness, stubbornness &c (as aforesaid) as they are now.

When there was persons in our post who proved very deficient in qualification, trust &c, yet the committee even then esteemed it to be an absolute necessity that the steward &c should be preserved in their authority until they could get some more suitable in their places or else the family might perhaps have gone into much greater confusion than it did at that time.

It might be very convenient for every friend at his first entering into the service of this committee to inform himself thoroughly relating to the government of the family, the bill of fare, orders of the house &c, first being authorised and approved us by a minute of the quarterly meeting and the last well approved by a committee of the quarterly meeting. And if they appear yet to be sufficient and justly administered then they who are newly come upon the committee may with more ease reject the many undue complaints generally made to them upon such their first entrance by discontented parents &c and order them to come to the committee &c.

Notwithstanding the orders may be very reasonable and the bill of fare sufficient, yet except the persons who are under you be just in administering &c you cannot safely maintain the reputation of the house.

It may therefore be well to consider whether any reasonable man (who has perhaps many times been obliged to assert that he never gave less than the bill of fare allows to any who can dispense with it &c) would contract guilt upon his mind in keeping back any part of the poor's allowance when it is not at his charge and might get much trouble and an ill name for so doing.

116. [p. 142] Memorandum, 11 June 1726.

This day Thomas Smith having come to see his children &c walked about a little [and] offered to go upstairs when the maid was washing them, whom I [had] desired to come down. [I] said, he should not go into the school, they should rather be called down, though but just gone up. To which he replied, he would go up in spite of my teeth, and did. But the school master locked the door, so that he saw them not till they came down, when I told him, he brought them home but last first day, though they ought to have come the 7th day, wherefore he little needed to have seen them again so soon. He said, he would come to see them every day in spite of my teeth, if he had a mind for it, for it was a public house, which in the yard he repeated diverse times in the hearing of the servants. And was so abusive that I told him, I ought to have a beadle to keep such disorderly persons out of the house that such abuse might be prevented or else a constable to keep the peace. For which he told me, I was a saucy impudent fellow and deserved a constable myself. My wife told him, it was on 7th days when always they were cleaning. He replied, he had nothing to do that day. My wife told him, she thought he might spend his time better than here, especially since he saw them so lately. He said, she was a saucy, impudent hussy and he would come every day and see them too, if they were alive, and said, he would take them, he could maintain them himself, he valued none of us. He told me, I did not do my duty and was not a Christian. I desired he would make that out. He said, because I did not correct them myself but let that saucy slut do it, meaning Hannah [Newton], and in an insolent manner as he had not foot under other folks' table, and said anything [he] thought would provoke and aggravate; threatening what he would do and much of that sort.

117. [p. 143] Memorandum, 11 June 1726.

Having while upon duty in the school understand that Thomas Smith was below, I gave my attendance, the steward being gone out . . . When I appeared he immediately broached a whole flood of complaints about his sons being cruelly beaten, pretending that if they wanted an ounce or ½ of finishing their tasks were beat for it unmercifully. And exclaimed against the house by making it parallel to Egyptian servitude, saying, why should they be limited to such a time for their tasks, and not take their own time. The boy being asked if he was beat for such a thing confessed the contrary, whereupon I took occasion to observe that his vulgar and very abusive deportment before his own children was the readiest expedient to lessen our authority, by preserving in them that disposition which had all along and still would procure them more of the same. To palliate which, he pleaded affection, but in short I should sooner have taken it to be the spirit of gin. Then he bragged they should not stay here to be beat by that saucy slut, meaning Hannah [Newton]. Upon which the stewardess bid him take them just then & withal reminded him how capable [he was] of maintaining them. To which he replied, he had as much money as she before she came thither. And to show more of his incorrigible ill-nature in alarming the whole neighbourhood, added, he would have every one take their children away and let her go again to her tailoring. And all the while pretended religion, crying out, he was ashamed . . . friends should be guilty of such cruelty. But so little was he ashamed of his own behaviour that all the acknowledgement we could get from him was that he had not said or acted anything amiss, for what he said, withal threatening how he would immediately go complain and went away.
H.[enry] E.[lbeck]

118. [p. 144] Workhouse, 24 August 1726.

Having heard that Thomas Smith denied what he said at this house on 11 June last, these may . . . [in]form any friends as occasion requires that I heard said Thomas Smith give the abusive language in the yard to my master, mistress &c contained in the just paper; also the abuses to my mistress in my master's absence, written by the school master in the second paper. And at the same time Thomas Smith denied that he had said that it was no charity to maintain children and keep them at work and that he could prove we made them earn their livings, though he spoke it in our parlour when my master, mistress and I were present there and heard him say it, and therefore esteem it not be so strange that he should deny his unbecoming treatment now, [to] which I was an ear witness [and] was much worse than is made appear in writing.

He spoke so loud that the tenants looked out at their windows, which he perceiving raised his voice louder, by which it appeared he intended they should hear him. Vaunting about in a very unbecoming manner he seemed to lay a pretty great stress upon the authority that he had for what he did as he then said.

He reported diverse things at friends' houses that were not true, which tended to beget a wrong understanding in the minds of friends relating to them who, to the best of their understanding, have . . . honestly discharged themselves in their services in [the] said house.

The children's parents coming so often to the house & showing such disrespect, also being abusive before the children &c, has tended very much to hurting the said children in making them tattle and hold together in contriving false stories to make their parents uneasy, hoping thereby to get out of the house. And things of this nature have been the cause of the idleness, stubbornness and untractableness of the children of late. And notwithstanding they now do so very little work to what was formerly done, yet some parents are discontent, although the children can have done easily by noon if diligent. If any who have the oversight of those children will indulge them in their idle, vain minds . . . [they] may have a very easy place in that service, also their parents' good word, though much to the disadvantage of the children and a great [p. 145] loss to the house in spoiling their work &c. But whoever in that place are conscientiously concerned to prevent such disadvantage as aforesaid may be unduly treated except some good expedient be found to prevent.

The reasons of my writing this now is because in a short time I shall leave London.   Hannah Newton, copy

119. Brewing, 27 February 1727.

An instruction for brewing for two quarters and half of malt. For the first liquor just make it boil or just break and then cool in about one fourth of the cold liquor. And for the second liquor make it just break and cool in one third of the cold liquor. Mash twice for the first wort. Mash the first as stiff as you can and for the second . . . mash as much as will make up the length thee intends to draw. And for the small liquor thou may just make them ready to boil and cool in one fourth of cold liquor, except the last and make that pretty sharp.

120. [p. 146] A visit, 4 February 1727.

The friends went directly up into the workroom amongst the children and said, here is a parcel of little creatures, poor little creatures indeed. Oh, how they work and in their shirts too. Some of the friends held up their hands saying, oh, poor little creatures. One of said friends who has a grandchild in this house said to Edward (who looks after the children), thou needs not walk with a cane under thy arm, they work in fear enough without, and asked my wife, what was the reason that the boy had sore hands, saying that, he had no sore hands before he came here. Also told us that he was not grown any bigger, for she had took a measure on him when he came into the house.

One of the friends asked, how we dressed the herring when the children had them to dinner and how many do you give them. I heard you gave them but one herring each. We first told the friend how we dressed them, which they seemed to approve of very well. Then said, we gave the big children three herrings each, and the small children two or two & an half according to the bigness of the herrings. But the friend was not willing to tell who it was that reported it.

The friends being with my wife talking in the workroom, . . . sent for me. And in the meantime, when we were discoursing in the workroom, the boys and girls went down as they had done work and some of said children said below stairs that the friends who came to visit the house, being in the workroom, said, oh the poor little creatures, how they work in their shirts; they always work in fear to be sure. Also said, they were scolding with the steward and stewardess. The servant maids also heard of it as well as some of the rest of the family.

The child had only one sore finger when he went home, also was very clean, decent and in good order and got the rest of the sores at home. And esteeming ourselves obliged to say so in opposition to what was reported and likewise our speaking a little in what condition the child was sent to the house again with which we suppose the friend was displeased or otherwise might have been as agreeable in her visit as the other friends. The said friend said that, she took measure of the lad when he came into the house and thereby she could tell that he was not grown. But we think he has considerably, also the looks of the child may partly show whether he is grown or not.

He has been here almost one year.

121. [p. 147] Physic, juleps, salve, ointments &c for the family:

From 29 September 1711 to 29 September 1728	10s.	8d.
Ditto to 29 September 1713	13s.	10d.
Ditto to 29 September 1714, consumptions, agues, aged &c.	£2 8s.	3d.
Ditto to 29 September 1715, two jaundices, agues, consumption, aged &c.	£2 8s.	9d.
Ditto to 29 September 1716, jaundice, consumption, small pox	£1 15s.	9d.
Ditto to 29 September 1717, jaundice, small pox &c.	£1 9s.	4d.
Ditto to 29 September 1718, looseness, convulsions &c.	£2 3s.	4d.
Ditto to 29 September 1719, fits, consumption &c.	£3 15s.	10d.
Ditto to 29 September 1720, rheumatism, pains &c.	£4 6s.	7d.
Ditto to 29 September 1721, rheumatism, itch, consumption &c.	£3 15s.	5d.
Ditto to 29 September 1722, fits &c.	£2 17s.	3d.
Ditto to 29 September 1723	£3 13s.	10d.
Ditto to 29 September 1724	£3 3s.	11d.
Ditto to 29 September 1725, fits &c.	£2 10s.	3d.
Ditto to 29 September 1726, fits, strangury &c.	£1 7s.	9d.

Ditto to 29 September 1727, fevers, agues &c. £2 2s. 11d.
Ditto to 29 September 1728, small pox, fevers,
convulsions &c. £4 5s.

£43 9s.

£2 10s. 7d. per year.

122. [p. 148] To the committee, 1 February 1725.
Friends, Our salary in the year 1719 was £40 per year. We then applied to
the committee desiring they would advance our salary to £60 per year and
the said committee did acknowledge we did deserve it, yet desired we
would be easy with £10 per year being added to our salary at present,
esteeming it would be easier for them to advance £10 per year sometime
after, than to advance £20 at one time. So now it is near 5 years since,
therefore, [we] do hope the committee may not esteem our present
application hasty or unseasonable. The paper we gave to the committee
when we last applied was as follows:
To the committee, 8 February 1720.
Friends, It's not pleasant to use this to apply, yet think ourselves under a
necessity to let you understand that we are not thoroughly easy with our
present salary, it being now going on nine years since we came to serve the
committee and do find ourselves not worth above £5 more than when we
came into the house.
And what, with submission, we desire of the committee is that you
would please to advance our salary.
We make no private gains to ourselves unknown to you, either directly
or indirectly, but give up our whole time and understanding to serve you,
esteeming it's but our reasonable duty so to do and we have been here in
the very prime of our time.
[p. 149] And if you would please to look back and inspect the increase
of our business now to what it formerly has been, as also the trade brought
to the house with the income and gains thereon for this seven years last
past, likewise a considerable advantage accruing to the house, also to the
monthly meetings may easily appear in clothing the ancient friends and
children, though we could not have served you in this respect had we been
of other business than that which we were brought up to.
We do hope, when things as aforesaid are duly considered, our request
may not be thought unreasonable, for we intend well and endeavoured to
do accordingly and have always had a due regard in our minds to the
committee. And if we had saved considerably every year in your service
could not have been more diligent in order to make you and the family
entirely easy in all respects.
So friends, desiring we may be preserved faithfully in our trust whilst
we are in it, and you esteem us worthy thereof has been at times the
sincere desire of us who are with due respects willing to serve you in this
post. Richard and Sarah Hutton
Note: our salary are for the service of two persons.

123. [p. 150] Memorandum, to the committee about taking a steward.
In the year 1711 the committee was then in want of two in this post and

desirous that they might not be such as were necessitous persons or had miscarried in their own circumstances, no public friend whereby they might be drawn out of the service of the house, nor to have children or to have many to come after them which might prove chargeable to the house. At that time the committee seemed inclinable to conclude they might find it difficult to procure two persons that were suitably qualified that would give their whole time entirely to the service of the house.

Buying the wool right and getting the yarn well spun is what the preservation, also the profit of the trade, seems to depend [on] and such has been the difference of the trade for about 12 years last past to what it was formerly that I could, unknown to any, have (and do suppose out of that article only) made our salary more per year than what we now desire. And at the same time, notwithstanding that, the trade would have appeared very good to what it did formerly, as aforesaid.

Keeping the accounts regular and drawing out the bills, also balancing the said accounts every quarter, likewise receiving and paying all the debts belonging to the house requires time, care and diligence.

Clothing the family, both the aged and the youth, which is attended with many trifling articles which cause pretty much writing, also care and exactness in posting to each particular account in order to write out the monthly meetings' bills.

Buying the provision and managing the family, which is somewhat difficult, also attended with various perplexities [p. 151] as may reasonably be supposed where there are several resolute and discontented persons to be concerned with daily.

Note: our salary is for two persons who are accountable for the whole, and when difficulties of any kind doth attend fails not of coming to our lot. And if this committee sees meet to comply with what is now desired, which [we] do hope, when the aforesaid is well considered, may not be thought unreasonable, . . . do assure you that while we continue in the service of the house shall not desire any further advance of our salary for the future.   Richard Hutton

124. At a committee, 13 September 1725.

The steward having some years since applied to the committee to advance his salary to £60 per annum and now again made the like application, this committee, in consideration of his care and pains with respect to the trade and his wife's conduct and service in the family, do now agree to make his salary £60 per annum to commence from the 29 instant, himself and wife having assured us that they will not at any time hereafter ask any farther advance to said salary and that they will continue in their service so long as they live and are able.
Present: John Plant, chairman, Richard Crafton, Junior, John Vandewall, George De Horn, John Kitchinman, John Bull, Walter Coleman, John Spencer, Daniel Vandewall, Thomas Paris, Cornelius Taylor, Thomas Rhoades, John Whiting.

125. [p. 152] At a committee at the workhouse, 22 November 1714.
Present: Richard Greener, chairman, Samuel Morgan, Abraham Ford,

Henry Aldworth, Edward Burford, James Paris, John Davis, Josiah Martin, William Walker South, John West.

Whereas Richard Hutton, the steward, and his wife have laid before the committee the necessity of advancing their salary to £30 per year without which they cannot well content themselves, upon consideration the committee doth agree that £5 be given them at the end of the present year's service besides the £20 granted as a salary; and the committee is willing that £10 be added to the salary of £20 for the future. Copy.

126. At a committee at the workhouse, 14 February 1716.
Richard Collet, chairman, George Wingfield, Abraham Ford, William Kight, Arthur Crossfield, Thomas Crawley, Edward Burford, Thomas Harrison, Joseph Ingram, Samuel Morgan, John Burroughs, John West, William Emmott, Josiah Martin, Henry Aldworth, Richard Partridge, James Paris.
It's agreed for the future that the steward's wages be advanced to forty pounds per annum from last quarter day. Copy.
Without my application.

127. [p. 153] At a committee at the workhouse, 8 February 1720.
Present: John Stanbery, chairman, James Swain, Daniel Gurney, James Harle, John Russell, Thomas Harding, Daniel Vandewall, Charles Benson, William Hodgson, Thomas Underwood, John Lee, Thomas Sandon.
Agreed that the steward's wages be advanced to fifty pounds per annum to commence from 25 December 17[blank] last. Copy.
Then was reported a bond of trust was signed by the steward to James Harle and John Lee.
The last minute about the £60 per salary is in page 151 in this book, backwards &c [**121**].

128. [p. 154] Memorandum.
Josiah Withers came 17 June 1728, which is to 25 March 1729, 40 weeks, in which time he cost the house in provision, viz:
Victuals, fire, washing, &c at 2s. 6d. per week, £5
Schooling 40 weeks at 6d. per week, £1   £6
N.B. Rent, repairs, taxes and other incidents are
not included in the above charge.
His allowance for 40 weeks diet, schooling &c at 18d.
per week is £3
His earnings since he came, to 25 March 1729 in 31
weeks, 3 days on 100lb. of yarn at 2½d. £1 0s. 10d.   £4   0s. 10d.

The house finding cards &c, Lost   £1 19s. 2d.

129. Robert Withers came 15 July 1728, whose charge at
25 March 1729, being 36 weeks 6 days since he came at
2s. 6d. per week, £4 11s. 3d.
Schooling at 6d. per week to ditto time, 18s. 5d.   £5   9s. 8d.
N.B.: rent &c as above not included.

His allowance for said 36 weeks 6 days maintenance, schooling &c. £2 15s. 3d.

His earnings to 25 March 1729 since he came, being 28 weeks 3 days on 47lb. of yarn at 2½d., 9s. 7½d.   £3   4s.   10½d.

The house finding cards, wheels &c, lost   £2   4s.   9½d.

130. I think the bigger of these two boys is 16 years of age and . . . when such are taken into the house who frequently have been used to sauntering about at a loose rate &c, then parents perhaps see nothing but ruin [p. 155] to their children without restraint and some education. And it seems to be [no] small difficulty to bring such children to any agreeable behaviour and especially to love improvement in business which appears not to be the design of their being sent in, by the earnest desires of their friends, for their being pushed forward in learning &c for which they were sent, as they say, also because they were to stay in the house but a little till qualified, then hopes I would endeavour to get them good masters when they should go out &c. It would scarcely be credited what trouble the man &c who looks after such (old, wrong managed) children at work is [at] bringing them to do the one half of that which we know well they could do with pleasure if industrious. And if any sharpness be used to bring such children out of bad habits as aforesaid then they complain and are uneasy and are minded, then it doubles the difficulty of . . . getting any thing done as usual by several of the children. And if a person who has the care of said children's work will be as vain amongst the children as themselves are, suffering them to spoil the work and when idle &c, throw the work back again into the pile of wool undone. Such a man will have no uneasiness from parents &c. I have a man now in the third year in that service to whom I have made everything as agreeable as I could & by his faithfulness and diligence in getting the work well done, the goods have been got off beyond expectation, which I do conclude we have great reason to be thankful to providence for considering the large quantity of yarn now on hand. But now this young man is about going into the country being quite tired, esteeming [the] perplexities he goes through at home with said children as well as abroad about them to be hurtful to him both in body and mind. Though in other respects he never expects a place so agreeable, yet for the reasons aforesaid together with confinement &c would not stay at any rate. [p. 156] And except some persons [be employed] who will be honest and industrious and have strength of body with a good disposition and a suitable resolution, your trade will be in danger, which though it may please some, yet do conclude the maintaining so many little helpless children at so small an allowance as 12d. per week, especially when provisions are at an advanced price as for a considerable time has been and though as formerly when the children spun more than now, and few spun it in town, yet the children's work was reckoned at 12s. per week as may be seen in the account given in, and we reckon the same now, and if this small income be lost, it may cause an unexpected running out every year. There is upwards of £9 lost this quarter, which would have been £20 or upwards could we have got all the

debts contracted this quarter ready to charge &c. And when the reputation & success which has attended the house for several years is rightly considered doubt not but all well minded friends will desire sincerely that it may providentially be preserved in that reputation which it has gained & still continues amongst several men of note who desire the welfare of said house and of friends in general though not of our society. Also that it may not yearly diminish the stock which formerly was a considerable discouragement to friends in general who had been at the great industry and charge of the first settlement and was supposed to prevent legacies being left because legacies did frequently drop in as soon as the house increased in stock &c the said suppositions seems reasonable.
19 May 1729, or then about &c.

131. [p. 157] Memorandum, 14 June 1729.

Nathaniel Clark in the year 1712 was in a manner quite blind, which was caused by convulsions in his eyes when a child, which yet continue, also made the couching of his eyes (though twice) lose the desired effect. He has for several years been very liable to be unwell and his life has been in danger; we were likewise afraid he would not have had the use of his feet as usual which was supposed to be the effect of the said fits.

If anything happens disagreeable to him it will soon put him out of order, which the fits as aforesaid are supposed to be the cause of, and if not carefully managed according to skilful advice, also supplied with proper medicines, which have been chargeable in times past, might have proved very uncapable of doing any business before this time.

He has been in the house near 17 years, came in at the allowance of 3s. per week (as the ancient friends did). Held there near 2 years at 2s. 6d. and 2s. about 4 years longer and since, to 29 September next, will be eleven years at 1s. 8d. per week. And it is now near 6 years since he has had £4 per year to buy him clothes for the easing the meeting's charge and for his encouragement which we hope may tend to preserve cheerful in his mind, which to be is supposed a great help against fits.

We had an ancient man at 4s. per week who brewed, kept the cellar clean, drawed drink &c and another at 3s. per week who also brewed, drawed drink &c & went errands & carried yarn & did what No. 6 does now. And the committee allowed the diligent should have encouragement & the monthly meetings expect the poor should be serviceable in the family which was agreeable to the directions of the great meeting, also to the orders of the house &c, for if there were not some helpful persons in the house how could the family subsist with the aged, blind, lame, bedridden &c of which some have frequently been in the house belonging to the respective monthly meetings.

132. [p. 158] London, 30 May 1683.

Dear friends, We received the letter and understand the case of the children and also the several precedents quoted to us & also what you say concerning the 18th of Leviticus. But you seem to take no notice of these words in the 6th verse: Thou shall not approach to any of thy near kin. Now, how near will the question be? The advice of friends . . . last year was to forbear marriage till the 4th degree was out. Now you know that father & mother is the first, brother and sister the second, their children the third, & the children's children is the fourth, which the civil law calls second cousins & is thereby forbidden, though not first cousins. Most men believe that those men who . . . met to make that order never thought first cousins would offer to marry, or else would doubtless have forbidden the first as well as the second. So to return to the law of God, which is expressly not to marry any near of kin, which is those of blood.

Now our sense is the blood of the kindred is not out in the sense of the law, either of God or man, till the fourth degree be past, for in the 17th verse there is prohibition of affinity in the third degree. [p. 159] Where there is no blood is yet called near kindred & declared to be wickedness to marry in that degree. So, dear friends, keep to the pure power of God, that keeps all pure & holy, sweet and acceptable to God & answers the life in his people by which the pure unity is preserved amongst you & the whole body of Christ. In his power you will be able to rule the affections & subdue them & break all snares whatsoever [that] are or may be laid for the innocent. Inwardly & outwardly in the fellowship of his power we give you this our tender advice & council, which you may communicate to the young people, your children & friends concerned with you about this matter. So, with our love to you all, from your friends in the truth.
George Fox, Leonard Fell, Robert Lodge, Stephen Crisp, James Park, John Banks.

133. [p. 160] Bishop Tillotson in the 11th sermon of the 7th volume of that part of his works printed after his death from page 324 to the end of said sermon tells us:

It is an observation of Sir Edwin Sands that as children are pleased with toys, so saith he, it is a pitiful and childish spirit that is predominate in the contrivers and zealots of a ceremonious religion. I deny not but that very honest and devout men may be this way addicted but the wiser any man is the better he understands the nature of God and of religion, the further he will be from this temper.

A religion that consists in external and little things, doth most easily gain upon and possess the weakest minds, and whoever entertains it, it will enfeeble their spirits, and unfit them for the more generous and excellent duties of Christianity. We have but a finite heat, and zeal, and activity, and if we let out much of it upon small things there will be too little left for those parts of religion which are of greatest moment and concernment. If our heat evaporate in externals, the heart and vitals of religion will insensibly cool and decline.

How should we blush who are Christians, that we have not learnt this easy truth from the gospel, which even the light of nature taught the heathen: [. . .] the best, the surest, the most chaste and most devout worship of the gods is that which is payed them with a pure sincere and uncorrupt mind, and words truly representing the thoughts of the heart. [. . .] Serve God with a pure, honest, holy frame of spirit, bring . . . a heart that is but generously honest, and he will accept of the plainest sacrifice.

And let me tell you that the ceremonious worship of the Jews was never a thing in itself acceptable to God, or which he did delight in, and though God was pleased with their obedience to the ceremonial law after it was commanded, yet antecedently he did not desire it; but that which our saviour saith concerning the law of divorce is true likewise of the ceremonial, that it was permitted to the Jews for the hardness of their hearts, [p. 161] and for their proneness to idolatry. God did not command it so much by way of approbation as by way of condescension to their weakness. It was because of a hardness of their carnal hearts that God brought them unto the law of a carnal commandment as the apostle calls it. See Psal. 51:16, 17; Jer. 7:21.

The reason why I have insisted so long upon this is to let you understand what is the true nature of Christ's religion. [And to abate the intemperate heat and zeal which men are apt to have for external, indifferent things in religion.] The sacrifices and rites of the Jews were [very unagreeable and unsuitable to] the nature of God; Psal. 50:13. Will I eat the flesh of bulls, or drink the blood of goats? Spirits neither eat nor drink. It was a very unsuitable way of service to kill oxen and sheep for God, and there's the same reason of all other rites which either natural necessity or decency doth not require . . . [Can] any man in earnest think that God, who is a spirit, is pleased with the pompous bravery and pageantry which affects our senses? So little doth God value indifferent rites, that even the necessary external service of God, and outward reverence, where they are separated from spirit and truth, from real holiness and obedience to the indispensable laws of Christ, are so far from being acceptable to God that they are abominable: nay [if] they be used for a cloak of sin, or in opposition to real religion, and with a design to undermine it. God accounts such service in the number of the most heinous sins.

You, who spent the strength and vigour of your spirits about external things, whose zeal for or against ceremonies is ready to eat you up, you, who hate and prosecute one another because of these things, and break the necessary and indispensable commands of love, as an indifferent and necessary ceremony, go and learn what that means. I will have mercy and not sacrifice, which our saviour doth so often inculcate, and that Rom. 14:17. The kingdom of God is not meat and drink &c. And study the meaning of this, God is a spirit, and they that worship him, must worship him in spirit and in truth.[1]

1. John Tillotson, *The works of the most Reverend Dr John Tillotson, late Lord Archbishop of Canterbury: containing two hundred sermons and discourses* (2nd ed., 1717) i, 754–5. Words etc. in square brackets appear in the text but not in Hutton's excerpt.

134. [p. 162] To fine a 30 gallon cask of strong beer or ale.
Take about 2 ounces of the finest & clearest isinglass beat or cut very small, put it into an earthen vessel with as much vinegar (or alligar) as will cover the isinglass. Brush it very well with a whisk twice or thrice a day till it be quite dissolved & as it grows thick put a little more vinegar to it till it becomes a very thick syrup, then strain through a cloth about a pint thereof (or more if over thin), then open the bung of the cask. With a

whisk then pour in the strained isinglass, stirring it very well also & bung the cask very close & in 24 hours your drink will be very clear . . . So in proportion may fine any greater or less quantity, but be sure when you put those things into the drink that you make everything so close as that you cannot draw any at the tap without first making a vent at top, lest your drink grow flat. Copy.

135. [p. 163] At a committee held at the workhouse of the people called Quakers at Clerkenwell, 19 May 1729.

John Jennings reports that Jacob Harvey Esq. is ready to pay the remainder of Elizabeth Clay's legacy left to this house. The steward is ordered to receive the same and give him a receipt as usual.

Received the [blank] of July 1729 of Mary Harvey, wife of Jacob Harvey Esq., executor to Elizabeth Clay's deed, the sum of twenty eight pounds seven shillings & six pence, which together with the sum of twenty eight pounds received 23 January 1724 & the sum of seven pounds ten shillings received 12 August 1726 (for which two last sums receipts have been already given) make the sum of sixty three pounds, seventeen shillings & six pence, being in full of a legacy left by the said Elizabeth Clay to the workhouse at Clerkenwell belonging to the people called Quakers. I say, received for the use & by order of the committee of the said workhouse.
By me, Richard Hutton.

136. [pp. 164–6. A rough draft of a paper discussing conditions in the house, Hutton's problems with various residents, and offering possible solutions to those problems. See **141**.]

137. [p. 167] N.B.: from 25 March 1717 to 25 March 1719
From No. B[1]

Day	Month	Year	Page	Ch[il]d	Week[s]	Earned	Gained
24	June	1717	396	34	8	£13 12s.	£23 7s. 6d.
29	Sept.		397	39	9	£17 11s.	£28 8s. 9¾d.
25	December		399	40	8	£16	£35 6s. 3¼d.
25	March	1718	438	33	9	£14 17s.	£32 13s. 11¾d.
24	June		439	30	8	£12	£24 16s. 2¾d.
29	Sept. . . .		483	29	9	£13 1s.	£27 7s. 6d.
25	December		497	34	8	£13 12s.	£24 18s. 10d.
25	March	1719	104	33	9	£14 17s.	£14 10s. 10¼d.
24	June		140	33	8	£13 4s.	£19 1s. 2½d.
29	Sept.		152	41	9	£18 9s.	£36 14s. 5¾d.
25	December		160	34	8	£13 12s.	£28 11s. 7½d.
25	March	1720	167	37	9	£15 3s.	£23 8s. 6d.
24	June		176	36	8	£14 8s.	£22 4s. 8d.
29	Sept.		180	43	9	£19 7s.	£41 8s. 11½d.
25	December		196	47	8	£18 16s.	£54 0s. 6d.
25	March	1721	201	40	9	£18	£32 14s. 7d.
24	June		226	45	8	£18	£39 8s. 8¼d.
29	Sept.		236	51	9	£22 19s.	£56 15s.
25	December		264	57	8	£22 16s.	£56 9s. 10d.
25	March	1722	275	50	9	£22 10s.	£20 17s. 0½d.

24	June		304	50	8	£20		£38	5s.	5d.
29	Sept.		311	58	9	£26	2s.	£56	0s.	3d.
25	December		321	56	8	£22	8s.	£55	9s.	6½d.
25	March	1723	302	47	9	£21	3s.	£46	11s.	3½d.

From No. C[1]

24	June		121	44	8	£17	12s.	£49	0s.	8¼d.
29	Sept.		134	42	9	£18	18s.	£55	12s.	1½d.
25	December		137	37	8	£14	16s.	£45	5s.	0¾d.
25	March	1724	143	34	9	£15	6s.	£41	8s.	1¾d.
24	June		148	29	8	£11	12s.	£31	16s.	1d.
29	Sept.		153	31	9	£13	19s.	£42	12s.	11¼d.
25	December		160	32	8	£12	16s.	£39	14s.	8¼d.
25	March	1725	163	34	9	£15	6s.	£28	17s.	6d.
24	June		173	38	8	£15	4s.	£31	14s.	
29	Sept.		190	41	9	£18	9s.	£45	14s.	9d.
25	December		203	44	8	£17	12s.	£43	16s.	5½d.
						£593	17s.	£1295	4s.	1¼d.

1. FSSWA, 'Ledgers B, C'.

138. [p. 168] From No. D[1]

Day	Month	Year	Page	Ch[il]d	Week[s]	Earned			Gained		
25	March	1726	203	42	9	£18	18s.		£32	9s.	1d.
24	June		217	43	8	£17	4s.		£24	2s.	4½d.
29	Sept.		247	48	9	£21	12s.		£38	10s.	9¼d.
25	December		250	48	10	£24			£31	4s.	3d.
25	March	1727	259	49	9	£22	1s.		£29	15s.	4½d.
24	June		252	51	6	£15	6s.		£22	0s.	1½d.
29	Sept.		129	54	11	£29	14s.		£30	19s.	10¼d.
25	December		119	54	10	£27	11s.	10d.	£34	18s.	0¼d.
25	March	1728	123	55	10	£27	10s.		£25	0s.	7d.
24	June		130	56	8	£22	8s.		£32	15s.	6¾d.
29	Sept.		145	57	11	£31	7s.		£34	16s.	4¼d.
25	December		149	55	10	£27	10s.		£30	4s	4d.
25	March	1729	158	52	9	£23	8s.		£25	15s.	10¾d.

		£308	9s.	10d.	£392	12s.	7d.
Brought forward	£593	17s.	£1295	4s.	1¼d.
	£902	6s.	10d.	£1687	16s.	8¼d.
gained	£1687	16s.	8¼d.
earned	£902	6s.	10d.
years – 12	£2590	3s.	6¼d.

1. FSSWA, 'Ledger D'.

139. [p. 170: there is no page 169.] A physician communicates this well experienced recipe for destroying bugs, with which he entirely cleared his own beds &c five years ago, and has told it to scores of families since, who have all found the same effects by it and never saw a bug afterwards.

Take of the highest rectified spirit of wine (viz. camp spirits that will burn all away dry, and leave not the least moisture behind[)] half a pint; newly distilled oil or spirit of turpentine, half a pint; mix them together and break into it, in small bits, half an ounce of camphor, which will dissolve in it in a few minutes. Shake them well together, and with a sponge, or a brush dipped in some of it, wet very well the bed or furniture wherein those vermin harbour or breed, and it will infallibly kill and destroy both them and their nits, although they swarm ever so much. But then the bed or furniture must be well and thoroughly wet with it, (the dust upon them being first brushed and shook off) by which means it will neither stain, or soil, or in the least hurt the finest silk or damask bed. That is, the quantity here ordered of this curious, neat, white mixture (which costs about a shilling) will rid any one bed whatsoever, though it swarms with bugs. Do but touch a live bug with a drop of it and you will find it to die instantly . . .

140. [p. 171] Having thus at large shown, both from the reason of things and from the practice of men, that the nature or essence of sin consists in a man's suffering himself to be drawn away by the enticements of some appetite, passion or interest, to do what he is sensible is not in itself fit and right, nor agreeable to the will and laws of God; the inference I shall now proceed to draw from this doctrine are briefly as follows:

1st. If every man is then only tempted to sin when he is drawn away of his own lust and enticed, the first evident inference from hence is that made by the apostle himself in the words preceeding my text: let no man say, when he is tempted, I am tempted of God. In the reason of things and in the nature of a moral government over the world, there must be proper trials of obedience and disobedience; which the goodness of God does not oblige him to remove because without such trials God's government of the world could not be at all a moral government over rational creatures. But God never tempts any man with design to draw him into sin. Nor will He suffer men to be tempted above what they are able. But will, with the temptation, also make a way to escape, that they may be able to bear it. 1 Cor. 10:13.

2d. No man can, with just reason, lay the blame of his vices upon that nature wherein God has created him, or upon those frailties he may be supposed to have derived from his first parents. For men are not accountable for the appetites of nature, nor for its infirmities any further than they suffer their own wills to be drawn away irregularly, contrary to the reason of things and to the laws of God.

3rd. No man can justly excuse his own wickedness by alleging that he was tempted by the devil. For the devil has no power to tempt men . . . otherwise than as wicked men tempt one another, by suggesting to them the allurement of pleasure and profit. Judas was covetous and a thief, Joh. 12:16, before Satan entered into him to betray his Lord for money. [p. 172] Ananias' crime likewise, Acts v. 3, was not extenuated, but aggravated, by his suffering Satan to fill his heart with deceitfulness and fraud. The prince of the power of darkness, Eph. 11:12, is a spirit that worketh only in the children of disobedience. And the strong delusion that permits him to send upon the world is nothing but the deceivableness of unrighteousness in them that love not the truth, but the devil & who give not place in Him. By yielding to sin He will flee from them, Joh. 4:7, Eph. 4:26, 27, 1 Pet. 5:9. And whosoever keepeth himself, that is guards himself against sin, we know that the wicked one toucheth him not, Joh. 14:30. And of every sincere mind it may in proportion be said in a lower degree, that he finds in it nothing to lay hold upon. This was the security of Abraham. His own heart was perfect with God. And had God in that case permitted Satan to deceive him, where there was not corrupt disposition in his own heart, the deceit had been inevitable, and Satan in that circumstance had not been Satan, but an instrument only in the hand of providence. And the security of every good man is in proportion the same. God will not suffer him to be tempted above what he is able, nor to be deceived where he is not drawn away of his own lust and enticed. Clark 8th vo-35 page.

141. [p. 173] Our last bill of fare, made in the year 1713 & 1714, considerably exceeds the former bill of fare in quantity, also in goodness of the provisions. And some time afterwards the trade of the house was better than formerly it had been and it was not long after before legacies began to drop in more than usual so that the house began to increase in stock, which was soon known abroad and was very agreeable to many friends who knew it or heard of it. But this did not long please all, for in the first place when our family heard of it I was told by some of them and in a very untoward and reflecting manner, saying, we hear that the house begins to save money by the poor, also said, that friends gave not their money to the house with that intent but it was in order that it might be laid out upon the poor to comfort them, and not to be hoard up &c. And in a small time afterwards these kind of reflections was heard abroad relating to pinching the poor and overworking the children &c and that thereby the house saved money every year as aforesaid. These things are observed to show that notwithstanding the provision may be ever so good, and the allowance plentiful yet if our stock increase several of the poor have been liable to conclude that they have not been well used &c, likewise dissatisfaction too frequently appears in the children's parents &c. And it is observable that while there are reporters at home also hearers and encouragers of reports abroad, the house may be liable to be injured in its reputation.

[p. 174] And it has likewise been observed that some of our society who may not have been altogether so agreeable or skilful in their sentiments relating to managing affairs of this nature and notwithstanding that, have been incident to be displeased if their requests or proposals are not complied with and before such who have for several years sincerely & industriously laboured for the good of the house. And through the goodness of providence said house has generally in the most difficult times been favoured with many who have been skilful, industrious and hearty friends to it as aforesaid. But with submission it may notwithstanding this still be feared that while there may [be] a disagreeable and discontented family at home, also too many more incident to hear and give credit to bad reports a reasonable consideration, so . . . thereby the reputation of the house may be lessened.

Hitherto a remedy has not been found to prevent the aforesaid disadvantages which appear so evident that it need no proof because the house has and still doth suffer thereby. But if . . . an agreeable understanding could be come into which might find out a means to accomplish so good an end, [it] might possibly produce these good effects, viz: thankfulness and content in the family, the interest and reputation of the house, also more quietness of mind to such who . . . may have the care or managing the affairs of it &c.

To keep in good order a family made up partially of men and women who are aged and too liable to be discontent, also boys and girls whose parents or other relations . . . has and yet may give much uneasiness, seems to be very [p. 175] difficult to keep in good order as just now observed.

To prevent or somewhat amend the aforesaid disorders which yet may and it's to be feared has been some disadvantage to the house already as aforesaid and in order thereunto it seems, with submission, absolutely necessary to have persons to serve the committee in this trust and government of said house who ought to be such who may be confided in. And when the committee together with the monthly meetings do conclude that they have conscientious persons to serve the committee in their trust who are just not with respect to the committee only, but to the poor of the family also, because doing right by the poor has generally by some been the matter in question.

When the meetings as aforesaid do conclude that they have such persons in this post as may be depended on as such who manage with as much prudence as they are capable, also with regard to justice in their trust in all respects, may it then seem agreeable to the monthly meetings to unanimously discourage such weak and unskilful persons as aforesaid, who by hearing reports give encouragement to the reporters not considering how indirect it is for reports to be brought to them who are persons altogether unconcerned when at the same time it is the care, also practice, of each monthly meeting to choose suitable friends for their representatives in the committee before whom all complaints may be laid heard and if just, redressed, under whose care it is to visit the house to see that things be kept in good order and may be thereby capable to give quarterly or monthly meetings an account thereof as occasions may require in order to preserve a good understanding betwixt the said meetings and the house.

[p. 174: page numbers 174 and 175 are repeated in the original pagination.] And if the said meetings might esteem it convenient to be very hearty in discouraging such who may incline to hear reports by renewing general cautions in the monthly meetings &c from one time to another when reports are spread abroad, it may be a means to discourage such who may be incident to report what may be told them, and that before the persons who may be the subject of such reports are inquired of to know whether they are true or not. And though it may be hoped that there may be many friends who mind not such reports, yet it may reasonably be supposed that diverse honest friends who may like the house very well have been imposed on and made very uneasy thereby. And if such things could be amended do hope that it might make the family more settled easy and thankful and consequently thrive better in body and mind.

And when the reputation of the house is thoroughly settled and carefully kept up from time to time, notwithstanding the false reports or evil surmisings which hath hitherto been, it may yet be hoped that for the future the monthly meetings may not have so much labour and exercise in prevailing with their poor to accept of so plentiful a maintenance but rather to advise or admonish them to walk worthy of so comfortable a provision that may fitly be compared to an estate which they can neither spend nor lose.

142. [pp. 175–7. A selection of accounts covering clothing, victualling, profit and loss, and legacies for selected years between 1718 and 1732.]

143. [p. 178] 1721.
Ed. H. Said thou and thy wife are brave folks indeed, and much valued. This great undertaking has had great success under your management. Providence has wonderfully blessed your endeavours, and though some of the most noted amongst friends (named several) very much exerted themselves in managing said affair, but had not the desired success and that it should take such a happy turn in your hands seems very remarkable, which makes you at present esteemed much.

But notwithstanding in process of time you may expect that there may kings rise up that knew not the affliction of Joseph and then perhaps your labours may not be much more valued than ours who took much pains though had not the desired success.

144. [p. 179] For weak eyes.
Take a new laid egg while it's warm and boil it hard that the yolk may be clear separated from the white. Then take a clean cloth & put the white of the egg in it (and let none of the yolk be in it). Then with clean washed hands squeeze it pretty hard & there will come out of the white about a spoonful of water, if it be right done. Then drop two or three drops of that water into each eye at night in bed & one hour before the person rises in the morning & at noon if the sight be very weak. Always observing to keep the eyes shut half an hour after the drops is put in. In cold weather the drops must be a little warm (because all cold things are hurtful to weak eyes). Put as many of the [drops] as will be used at one time into a clean spoon & hold it towards a clear fire till the cold is just off. Keep the egg water in a cool place in hot weather & when it begins to alter in the smell, get fresh & use the old no more because the old will do harm. The best way to drop it into the eye is with a pigeon feather, they being small at the end.

Be careful never to use it if it be not sweet & no egg will do but one that is new laid and warm.

145. [p. 180] As the just performance of every office in a community ought to be not only the chief subject of their consideration who are deputed thereto but also managed according to the direction of the dispensing power, so it is but reasonable and just that they should in cases of difficulty have recourse to that authority whereunto they are accountable.

Seeing therefore that [the] grappling circumstances the house now struggles under for her reputation require your weightiest thought, I shall give you herein a detail of her present grievances, and with submission to your judgement what dangerous consequences, in my apprehension, may of all probability attend the toleration and indulgence of their authors.

But as my time in your service has not been long so perhaps it may not be productive of as many specimens of ingratitude and discontent as that of some others before me, yet I am of opinion I can upon the challenge meet them with uncommon instances of both, though indeed the plurality of your pensioners may indifferent be excepted from either, provided they have the utmost stretch of that liberty that your orders allow them. But in consideration of the privileges providence has here possessed them of under so just an administration no wonder the actions express the last degree of thankfulness and peaceable behaviour, the contrary whereof has of late been too much the unhappiness of some and still is, but especially amongst the women whose mutual jars and contention sufficiently tell us how insensible they are of the good design of those accommodations where with they might spin out a happy old age.

[p. 181] I need not here put the affront upon your memories to produce every example of misconduct hinted at, the various writings already laid before you giving sufficient proof thereof.

But to come to the subject of all our hardships, the great and most palpable grievance which now seems to crave your attention is the unnecessary communication of parents with children at the house . . .

1. How unnecessary it is (no extraordinary occasion as sickness &c requiring it) I am of opinion you will not long be unsensible, not only at the expense of your trade but the reputation of every important service in the family unless remedied by your unanimous endeavours. For the time of their going home with the two-fold learning and moderate exercise, privilege of their education, considered . . . they doubtless are unparallel with many in the circumstances. Nay this I know, that many children and young men of much better fashion than this house generally affords have, do and doubtless will, live at such a distance from their parents as not to see them some years together during which abdication they have approved themselves more manly and studious than whilst under the caresses of an unweaned and frivolous affection. And should these maintained on your charity claim greater indulgence than they? Nay, they have it and are not content . . . which is . . . [considered] really unpardonable . . . [by] all our modern [p. 182] as well as ancient masters of education. For we cannot place these who must expect a livelihood from their own labour and industry on an equal level with those who [have] the advantage of a more liberal education.

2. The sad consequence of such communication have doubtless been too notorious to escape your notice wholly. For as there is in all children a propensity to endure no restraint, evade their known duty & readily . . . to embrace any means for that very purpose, so by the success we are eye witnesses they have, we are certain their parents contribute no little to the

strengthening that disposition, giving ear to their partial tittle-tattle against your servants and the quibbling and false reports of their work &c, which with their own abusive and unmannerly treatment of us and the contempt they have shown of the house has been enough to pattern them into their disorder; for what can teach them readier than example. Nor must it be here omitted that such children as at their first coming have been modest and well inclined (though they have had no parents living or such as were orderly and respectful) have notwithstanding our endeavours to the contrary been exampled into the same practices. Besides who can pass by those dangerous habits of spoiling or neglecting their work. They is faithful in your service without reasonable resentment though it be to the hazarding their reputation, for diverse there are and not of the meanest sort who being too [p. 183] credulous have through partial information been beguiled with prejudice against our management.

Another misfortune attends this undue treatment we have often put up with, which has within the verge of my short time been too obvious, is that servants, apprentices &c hearing and seeing their master and mistress so contemptuously and lightly treated and the house abused without any so much as formal censure passed upon their repeated insults – having by . . . some buddings of ill manners already shown how far they copy after them. Nay, can't it be expected that they who ought to be so immediately under the dictate and regard of their governors as apprentices &c can pay that due respect and deference to them, when they themselves see such flagrant instances of abuse . . . still continued as if unresented.

But considering the many workhouses now in the city and suburbs partly upon the same business with yours you will find such disorders strike at the very root of her reputation.

So that not only the support of us in our respective duties as well as the reformation of manners but also the very basis of your establishment now requires your speedy succour which in my apprehension you cannot contribute to until all communication of parents with children at the house be entirely cut off (except in case of sickness or the like) by a firm order to the contrary.

And as you have formerly succeeded well in the removal of many grievances, so now we hope our joint endeavours to preserve that harmony and concord which . . . [p. 184] together with your concurrence is the best means to accomplish the design, will not now fall short of equal success against this last struggle and ultimate effort of common assailants.
1728   Henry Elbeck.

146. To the committee, 24 January 1732.
Friends, I desire you would please to take into consideration some methods as you may think fit about a new bill of fare or otherwise that there may for the future be no reflection cast upon the plentiful provision of the house, which may prove a great disadvantage to it, especially if any of your own members should appear dissatisfied in that respect. Besides the hard censures I and especially my wife may be liable to, having the managing said house under you, . . . we cannot possibly be easy except

you & the family are easy also, which always was great satisfaction to us, who desired to make you and the family easy, esteeming it but our reasonable duty.   Richard Hutton

147. [p. 185] At a committee, 9 October 1727.
Present Thomas How, Robert Deeklair, George De Horn, Robert Sherrwin, Thomas Rhoades, John Jennings, Thomas Paris, John Plant, Josiah Fooks, Richard Crafton, Thomas Baskervill, Thomas Reynolds.
This committee having frequent complaints of the great inconveniency of the children running away from this house and thereby taking the opportunity of telling diverse notorious lies to the prejudice of the same and scandalizing the government thereof, this committee therefore resolve it shall be a standing rule not to allow the steward to receive again any such child till the monthly meeting to which the child belongs request it. Copy.

148. At a committee, 17 April 1732.
John Barnard, John Gopsill, William Howard, Richard Robins, Benjamin Bell, William Cakly, Thomas Rhoades, Jacob Bell, John Jennings, Edward Wood, Anthony Neat, Jacob Foster, Thomas How, Cornelius Taylor.
It appearing to this committee that diverse reports have been spread of severity used by the steward and other servants in this house and on examining said reports they appear groundless, this committee therefore desires the members of it to discourage such reports as much as in their power. And when any complaints are made to them, to direct said complainers to attend the next committee in order to have . . . [p. 186] the said complaints heard and justly determined. This with the cautionary minute of 4 December 1727 to be continued to be read to every new member. Copy.

149. [p. 187. An account of money earned and gained from the manufacture of mop yarn between 1717 and 1725.]

ADDITIONAL DOCUMENTS

150. [FSSWA, 'Best Minutes, 1701–1708', f. 28]
A bill of fare brought in per Richard Hawkins, passed by the board and ordered to be entered and is as followeth [1702]:
Imprimis For [the] first day, in the morning: 4 ounces of bread and 1 ounce of butter and beer sufficient.
First day for dinner: 5 ounces of bread and 6 ounces of mutton and pottage each.
First day for supper: 4 ounces of bread & 2 ounces of cheese, or 1 ounce of butter.
A second day for breakfast: the mutton pottage well thickened with oatmeal and each, 4 ounces of bread.
A second day, dinner: a quart of peas between 4, either made into a pudding or pottage, 6 ounces of butter & 12 ounces of bread.
A second day for supper: 4 ounces of bread, 2 ounces of cheese, or 1 ounce of butter for each.
A third day for dinner: 5 ounces of bread and 6 ounces of beef & pottage for each.
A third day for supper: as second day for the same.
A fourth day: the same for breakfast as they have a third day.
A fourth day for dinner: furmenty, as much as is necessary & 5 ounces of bread each.
A fourth day for supper: the same as of [the] third day.
A fifth day: in all respects as of 3 days.
A 6 day, in the morning: as 3 days.
A sixth day for dinner: pudding peas, 9 ounces each.
Supper a sixth [day]: as other days.
Seventh day: water gruel for breakfast & bread as at other time.
Tripe for dinner. And for supper, as at other times.

151. [FSSWA, 'Standing Minute Book, 1701–1792, pp. 56–7]
A bill of fare for the family is as followeth, 4 August 1713.
Day 1st

Breakfast	Ancient friends: each 4 ounces bread, 2 ounces cheese, or 1 ounce butter & beer sufficient.
	Children: each 4 ounces bread, $1\frac{1}{2}$ ounces cheese, or 1 ounce butter & beer sufficient.
Dinner	Ancient friends: each 8 ounces roast meat without bones, 4 ounces bread & 1 pint beer.
	Children: big, each 8 ounces; small, each 6 ounces roast meat, 4 ounces bread & beer sufficient.

| Supper | Ancient friends: each the same as at breakfast. |
| | Children: each the same as at breakfast. |

Day 2nd

Breakfast	Ancient friends: each the same as on first days.
	Children: the same.
Dinner	Ancient friends: each 1 pint of milk, 4 ounces bread & beer if required.
	Children: each 1 pint of milk, well thickened with bread.
Supper	Each same as at breakfast.

Day 3rd

Breakfast	Each same as on second days.
Dinner	Ancient friends: Each 8 ounces boiled meat without bones, 4 ounces bread & 1 pint of beer.
	Children: big, each 6 ounces of meat; & to small, 4 ounces, with 1 pint of broth, 4 ounces of bread & beer sufficient.
Supper	Each the same as at breakfast.

Day 4th

Breakfast	Ancient friends: each one pint of broth, 4 ounces bread & 1 pint of beer.
	Children: each 1 pint of broth well thickened with bread.
Dinner	Ancient friends: each 1 pint of furmenty or rice milk, 4 ounces bread & 1 pint of beer.
	Children: each one pint of furmenty or rice milk with bread & beer sufficient.
Supper	Each same as third days' supper.

Day 5th

Breakfast	Each the same as on third days.
Dinner	Ancient friends: each 8 ounces boiled meat without bones, 4 ounces bread, 1 pint beer.
	Children: big, each 6 ounces meat & 1 pint broth; to small, each 4 ounces meat & 1 pint broth, 4 ounces bread and beer sufficient.
Supper	Each the same as at breakfast.

Day 6th

Breakfast	Each the same as on fourth days.
Dinner	Ancient friends: each one pound of plum or plain pudding & 1 pint of beer.
	Children: big, each 1 pound of pudding; and to small, each 12 ounces with beer sufficient.
Supper	Each the same as on fifth days.

Day 7th

Breakfast	Each the same as on fifth days.
Dinner	Ancient friends: each 1 pint of milk pottage with 4 ounces bread, or 1 pint of peas pottage & 1 ounce butter & 1 pint of beer.
	Children: 1 pint of milk pottage thickened with bread, or 1 pint of peas pottage with bread, butter and beer sufficient.
Supper	Each the same as at breakfast.

N.B. It is left to the discretion of the steward to diet the aged or sick as

may be thought convenient. And when peas, beans, mackerel, herring, salt fish &c are in season . . . [he may] change a meal or meals as shall seem necessary.
Absent persons must have no allowance.

152. [FSSWA, 'Standing Minute Book, 1701–92', pp. 91–2]
Orders to be observed by the ancient friends taken into this house.
1. That (except when the affairs of the family will not permit) you do at all times appointed, constantly attend the meetings for worship at this house on first and fifth day mornings, and at the Peel on first and third days in the afternoon, and return home in due season.
2. That you love one another as brethren and sisters of one family, making it your daily care to preserve a spirit of unity and patience amongst yourselves. And that you be tender hearted and ready at all times to help according to your strength such amongst you as are weak and feeble and stand in need of your assistance, (not knowing how soon it may be your own case), cheerfully performing whatever the steward shall require of you for the service of the family, according to your abilities. And also, that you do render to him an exact account of what money any of you shall earn, and pay the same into his hands.
3. That all who are able and in health, do attend constantly in the public dining room at meal times, and sit reverently at the table, otherwise, to have no victuals . . . And if at any time any person's allowance shall exceed what they incline to eat at a meal, such person or persons are to return what is left to the steward whilst it is fresh and good.
4. That if any be found carrying away, giving away, purloining or selling any part of their own allowance, or anything belonging to the house, or consenting to any others doing so, [they] shall, for the first offence, appear before the committee and be liable to what they shall see meet to do or order in that case. And for the second offence, [they] shall be expelled [from] the house.
5. That you carefully avoid contention, and in case any difference should arise you shall, before aggravations on either side are given, appeal to the steward and submit to his judgement therein . . . Otherwise, he shall lay the matter before the committee for them to determine the same as they see meet.
6. That none go out without the leave of the steward.
7. That no tobacco be smoked in anyone's lodging room.
8. That the family be all in bed by the eighth hour in the winter and by the ninth hour in the summer. And that none be up later, nor . . . any fire or candle be kept in anyone's room or chamber without leave of the steward.
The steward is hereby directed to see that these orders of the house be duly minded, and if any person shall refuse to observe them, that he do acquaint the committee therewith.
Agreed to by the committee 9 February 1719.

153. [FSSWA, 'Standing Minute Book, 1701–1792', pp. 93–4]
Orders to be observed by all the children taken into this house.

1. For the promotion of piety and godliness and the benefit of the family, it's ordered that all the children do constantly attend the meetings for worship at this house on first and fifth day mornings, and at the Peel on first and third days in the afternoon, and that they do frequently read the holy scriptures.

2. That about the fifth hour in the morning in the summer, and the sixth hour in the winter, upon ringing the bell, they rise, and after dressing themselves, washing their hands and face, combing their heads and brushing their clothes, for which half an hour . . . is allowed them, they shall then proceed to work. Each of them doing so much every day as the steward shall think fit and allot them. And that none to make any waste of their wool or anything else, nor suffer any with their consent or knowledge to . . . [do so], without informing the steward thereof or such other person as he shall appoint to oversee them in his absence. And that no noise or disturbance be seen or heard in the workroom.

3. That when the bell is rung to meals they shall, after washing themselves and brushing their clothes, go orderly to the table and, sitting down in their respective places, keep silent, shewing a good behaviour to all, of what rank soever. The school master and mistress to be present.

4. They shall not speak untruths nor use naughty words, but avoid idle discourse and use plainness of speech to all, as well as to each other.

5. They shall not break the walls or windows about the house, neither shall they strike one another or be quarrelsome, but of peaceable behaviour. But if any child thinks himself ill . . . treated or aggrieved by another, let him acquaint the steward or such other person who in his absence hath the oversight of them.

6. They shall not go out of the gate without leave.

7. The child who enticeth another into a fault is to receive double punishment, but if he or she that is drawn into the fault shall confess it before it's found out, they shall, in that case, find favour.

8. That once in every month these orders be read to the children that none may plead ignorance. And as often as any of them are broken, the steward is ordered to take care that they who break them have due correction for every offence.

Also the committee expects that the steward should give proper orders to the servants who have or shall have the care or oversight of the children at their work, that they do likewise take care to see them washed and dressed as is ordered in the second article. As also to see them quietly in bed at night and in general, that all the servants hired into this house be subject to the steward and stewardess as becometh them.

Agreed by the committee 9 February 1719.

154. [FSSWA, 'Standing Minute Book, 1701–1792', pp. 95–6]
The house queries &c at taking of ancient friends into the house.

1. We suppose thou desires to dwell in this house. Hast thou seen the orders or heard them read?

2. Art thou willing to observe them & comply with them?

3. Hast thou seen the bill of fare or heard it read?

4. Art thou well satisfied with it?

5. Thou mayst observe that the orders of the house oblige every friend to return what they don't eat of their provision to the steward whilst it is fresh and good . . . as the allowance in the bill of fare is more than the ancient friends can often dispense with. So we expect our orders should be punctually complied with by everybody. For, as it is our care there should be no want, so we expect there should be no waste.

6. Art thou able to dress and undress thyself, make thy own bed, keep thy chamber & clothes clean?

7. Hast thou thy health and art thou clear from any infectious distempers?

8. Hast thou paid thy just debts?

9. Formerly the ancient friends taken into this house were kept to work, but of late the committee has thought fit to excuse them from it in order to render them as easy as may be, and that everyone may have time and opportunity the better to lend a helping hand to each other when weak or ill, and cheerfully to perform what the steward shall require of them for the ease and service of the family, as well as for their own convenience, such as sometimes making a fire in the dining room (and the women friends to be assisting in mending the children's things). Art thou willing, cheerfully, to do according to thy ability what shall be so required of thee?

10. We expect the ancient friends should sit together at the meeting at this house in that part of it which the steward shall order according to our direction to him in that case.

11. We likewise expect that the ancient friends should be good examples of quietness and contentment to the children, as well as each other. And that nothing of [the] differences amongst them appear before the children. But if any should happen to arise, that they immediately compose it between themselves or apply to the steward in the children's absence, for him to determine or lay before the committee.

We shall give orders to the steward to take thee in, but thou must first be provided with the usual necessaries of bedding & clothes, of which he will give thee an account if thou apply to him.

155. [FSSWA, 'Standing Minute Book, 1701–1792', p. 97]

The several queries &c at taking of children into the house.

1. How old is this child?

2. Hath he had the smallpox?

3. Hath he his health pretty well?

4. Is he free from weakness or any catching distempers?

5. Is he not used to wet his bed? Some children having been attended with such like weakness, hath been an inconvenience to the family.

6. Hast thou seen the bill of fare or heard it read?

7. Because that is the steward's rule by which to diet the family, dost thou like it for the child as it is there ordered?

8. Well child, what dost thou say? Art thou willing to come and live here as the rest of the children do?

9. Thou must be sure to mind and please the steward and such as have the care and oversight of you. And you will be allowed proper season to play in.

We shall give orders to the steward to take the child in as soon as the necessaries are ready and sent in with him, of which he or the stewardess will give thee a particular account.

Children from the country &c.
It is the order of this house that if any child, not properly the monthly meetings's charge, be taken in and should happen to have the smallpox &c, the charge of physic, wine, a nurse and extraordinary fire & candle should be borne by the person who is engaged for the weekly allowance, which we expect thou will also comply with.

INDEX

Accounting *see* bookkeeping
accounts, 5, 10, 28–37, 47, 49, 63, 77, 83, 100, 103, 109, 111, 121, 128–31, 137–8, 142, 149, 152
acknowledgements, xix, 57–8, 88
Acts of Parliament
  11 Henry VII c.7, 16
  11 Henry VII c.15, 16
  23 Elizabeth c.1, 17, 20
  27 Elizabeth c.12, 16
  29 Elizabeth c.6, 17, 20
  3 James I c.4, 17, 20
  13 & 14 Charles II c.12, xiii
  30 Charles II stat.2, 17–21
  9 George I. c.7, xx
Albury, John, 110
Aldworth
  Ann, 14
  Henry, 126–7
  Richard, 15
alligar (alegar), 134
Allin, Abraham, 30
Amey, Thomas, 17
ancient friends, xiv, xvi, xix, xxi, 7, 23, 46, 54, 56–7, 59, 68, 72, 74, 80, 82, 87–8, 97, 104–6, 108, 131, 141, 145, 151–2, 154
Ansel
  John, 61
  Joseph, 61
Antrobus, Benjamin, 58
apprenticeship, 11, 37, 46, 68, 130, 145
arithmetic, 11, 42, 94, 107
assizes
  Appleby, 20
  Cambridge, 17
Atterwood, Edward, 30

Baker, Jacob, 17
Banks, John, 132
Barclay, Robert, 1
Barnard, John, 148
Barr, George, xv
Baskervill, Thomas, 147
Basnett, Richard, 16
Bates, Edward, 28
Beadle, Elizabeth, 58
beadles, 1, 16
Beard, Nathaniel, 110

Bell
  Benjamin, 148
  Jacob, 148
Bellers, John, viii–xiii, xv, xix, 90, 92
benefactions, ix, 46, 68, 105; *see also* legacies
Benson, Charles, 127
bill of fare, 7, 45, 68, 80–2, 88, 97–9, 104–5, 115, 120, 141, 146, 150, 154–5; *see also* diet
Bills, John, 62
Board of Trade, xii–xiii
Boehme, Jacob, 1
bonds, 127
bookkeeping, 1, 10–11, 89, 123
Booth, William, 90–1
Bostock, Henery, 17
Brady, William, 113–14
brewhouse, xv
brewing, 10, 49, 51, 73, 84, 95, 119
Bridewell Walk, xiv
Bristol, xix
Bull, John, 124
Bunhill Fields, vii
Burford, Edward, 26, 125–6
Burroughs, John, 126
Burton, Jonathan, 1
Byard, George, 30

Cakly, William, 148
Cambridgeshire friends, 17
camphor, 139
candles, 95, 155
capitalism, ix
Carr, Edward, 87
Cary, John, xii–xiii, xix
casks, 134
ceremony, 133
Chalk, Joseph, 2
charity, viii, 86, 108, 145
Chester, 62
Child, Sir Francis, xix
children, vii, xiv, xvii, xix, xxi, 84, 88, 104–5, 107–8, 113, 120, 122, 130, 132, 137–8, 141, 145, 147, 151, 153–5; *see also* education, employments
Christian-Love Poor, xxi
Claridge, Richard, 87

Clark
  Edward, 58
  Margrat, 58
  Nathaniel, 131
Clay, Elizabeth, 135
Clayton, Robert, xii
Clements Lane, vii
Clerkenwell, Quaker workhouse at, *passim*
  accommodation in, xiv–xv, 88, 99, 113;
    cellars, xiv; kitchen, 23, 39, 97, 113;
    pantry, 97; parlour, xiv, 86, 97, 118;
    stable, xv, 37, 49–50, 84; storeroom,
    xv; workroom, xv, 86, 120, 153
  committee, viii, xv, xviii, 7, 15, 25, 43–6,
    49, 57, 66, 72, 75–6, 80–1, 84, 88, 93,
    97, 99, 102, 104–6, 110, 115, 122–7,
    135, 141, 146–8, 152
  conditions in, xvii, 58, 66, 68, 80–2, 86, 97
  finances of, ix, xvi, xviii, 3, 9–10, 24, 37,
    46, 49, 51, 68, 93–6, 123, 130, 137–8,
    141, 154; *see also* accounts
  lease of, xiv–xv, 76, 90–2
  numbers in, 54, 58, 61, 68, 71–2
  orders and rules of, 23, 39, 68, 80–1, 88,
    98, 104–6, 113, 115, 147, 152–4
  repairs to, xv, 50–1, 77, 90–2, 100, 103;
    floors, 90; gutters, 103; plumbing, 103;
    roof, 90–1, 100, 103; sewerage, 90;
    windows, 103
  reputation of, 47, 56, 68, 80–1, 85, 88, 97,
    99, 104–6, 113, 115, 118, 130, 141,
    145–6
  servants in, 10, 23, 47, 72, 80, 82, 84, 88,
    97–8, 104–5, 107, 115–16, 120, 130,
    141, 145, 148, 153; *see also* Newton,
    Hannah
  steward, vii–viii, xv, xvi, 115, 117, 123,
    135, 141, 147–8, 152–5; duties of, 123;
    salary or wages of, xv, 24, 37, 43, 45,
    50, 82, 93–5, 122–7; *see also* Barr,
    George; Hutton, Richard; Powell,
    John; Trafford, Samuel
  stewardess, 153; *see also* Hutton, Sarah
  trustees, 90
  see also bill of fare, diet, employments,
    school
clocks, 63
cloth, 29; baize, 34; buckram, 31; canvas,
    31, 35; cotton, 93, 95; damask, 34, 139;
    Dowlass, 36; Dutch check, 29, 34; flax,
    viii n., x–xi, 96; fustian, 29; galloon, 31;
    garlic Holland, 29; genting, 32; glazed
    Holland, 31; Holland cloth, 36; kersey,
    29; lace, 34; linen, 23–4, 35, 54, 96;
    Russian cloth, 29–30, 32, 34; sack, 96;
    samplers, 24; serge, 31; shalloon, 31;
    silk, 31–2, 139; silk-worsted, 24; skins,
    29, 35; worsted, 94–5
clothing, 23, 28, 49–50, 54, 61, 72, 97, 122,
    131; aprons, 34; bodices, 31; body

linings, 33; bonnets, 34; breeches, 28–
    9, 35, 43; buckles, 31–2; buttons, 29,
    35; caps, 35; clogs, 31–2; girdles, 34;
    gloves, 30–2, 36; gowns, 33; handker-
    chiefs, 29–30, 34; hats, 30, 35, 50;
    hoods, 31–2; hooks and eyes, 29; man-
    tuas, 31; neckcloths, 29; pattens, 32;
    petticoats, 31, 33–4; shifts, 36; shoes,
    23, 30, 34–6; shoe buckles, 30; silk
    laces, 31; stay tape, 29, 31, 34–5; stays,
    34; stockings, 23, 30–2, 36; waistcoats,
    28–9; whalebone, 31
Clutton, Joseph, 1
coal, 10, 49, 51, 84, 87
Cobb, Eleanor, 82, 85, 87
Cockbill, Mary, 58
Coleman, Walter, 124
college of infants, xiv
Collet, Richard, 126
communism, viii–ix
complaints, xvii–xviii, 7–8, 39, 43, 66, 68,
    72, 74, 80–2, 84–8, 97, 99, 104–6, 113,
    115–17, 120, 141, 145–6, 148
constables, 16, 116
Constantine, John, 64
contracts, for supply of goods, 6
Conyers, John, 64
Cooke, Edward, 17
Cooper
  Daniel, 38
  Samuel, 28
co-operativism, viii–xii, xiv, xvii, xix–xxi
Corbet, Thomas, 16
Corporation Lane, xiv
corporations of the poor, xi–xv, xix, xxi
court leet, 16
Coxe, Thomas, 28, 50–1, 61
Crafton, Richard, 147
Crawley, Thomas, 126
Crisp, Stephen, 1, 132
Crossfield, Arthur, 126
Crow, Thomas, 14
Croydon, Surrey, xxi

Davis, John, 125
Deeklair, Robert, 147
De Horn, George, 124, 147
Denham, a tenant, 49
dictionaries, 11
diet, xiii, xvii, 4, 7, 59, 66, 68, 74, 80–1, 88,
    97, 104–5, 113, 120; beans, 151; beef,
    80–1, 86, 97, 113, 150; beer, xviii, 81,
    86, 104, 134, 150–1; boiled meat, 151;
    bread, 6, 50, 86, 99, 113, 150–1; bread
    pudding, 112–13; broth, 113, 151; but-
    ter, 50, 86, 104, 150–1; calves foot, 85;
    cheese, 50, 86, 104, 150–1; dumplings,
    82; figgy pudding, 82, 84; fish, 84, 111,
    113; furmenty, 4, 80, 84, 104, 150–1;
    gravy, 97; herring, 120; mackerel, 151;

meat, 39, 84–5, 97, 113; milk, 151; milk pottage, 4, 80, 113, 151; mutton, 80–1, 97, 113, 150; oatmeal, 150; peas, 150–1; peas pottage, 151; plum pudding, 4, 97, 151; pork, 80–1, 86, 113; pottage, 84, 150; pudding, 82, 84, 88, 97, 150–1; rice milk, 84, 104, 113, 151; roast meat, 151; salt fish, 151; spoon meat, 81, 104; sprats, 84; Suffolk cheese, 86; tripe, 150; veal, 113; water gruel, 104, 150; *see also* medicine
disorderly behaviour, 8, 43–5, 64, 80, 82, 84–5, 88, 97, 99, 102, 104–6, 110, 113, 115–18, 130, 141, 145, 147, 152–3
Dockura, Ann, 17
Doggett, Hannah, 13–15, 27, 49
Dolben, Sir William, 20
Durston, Edward, 1

East India Company, 26
East India stock, 26, 49, 51
education, ix, xvi–xvii, xix, 11, 23, 68, 95–6, 107–8, 118, 128–9, 145; of girls, 23; *see also* school
Edwards, Jonathan, 30
Elbeck, Henry, school master, 117, 145
Ellis, John, 90
embezzlement, 82, 85–6, 88, 123
Emerson, Francis, 17
Emmott, William, 126
employments, viii–x, xvi, xix–xx, 59, 72, 82, 84, 86, 93–4, 99, 104, 106, 108, 117–18, 120, 128–30, 145, 153–4; carding, xvi, 93; firing, 95; knitting, x; picking oakum, xvi; pin making, xix; reeling, 94; seamstry, 107; sewing, x, xvi, 23, 49, 52, 95, 107–8; shoemaking, xvi; spinning, x–xi, xvi, xix, 2, 24, 52, 93; winding silk, xvi; training and instructors for, 93–5
    contractors, 94–6; earnings from, 3, 37, 52, 94–6, 107–8, 118, 122, 128–30, 137, 138; wastage, spoiled work, 94–6, 104, 118, 130, 145; wheels, 96; work schedules, 23
English, 11
Everingham, Richard, 61
executors, 13–15, 26, 40, 76
exercise, 96
Exeter, 57

Farrier, 50
Fell, Leonard, 132
Field, John, 40–1
Firmin, Thomas, xi, xiii
Fleming, Sir Daniel, 20
Fooks, Josiah, 147
Ford, Abraham, 125–6
Forster, Josiah, 105

Foster
    Daniel, 61
    Jacob, 61, 148
Fox, George, x–xi, 132
France, 11
France, Grace, 2
Franck, August, 1, 70
Freame, John, 92

Gilbert, Thomas, xxi
Gorden
    Elizabeth, 64
    John, 8, 64
Gospill, John, 148
grammar schools, 11
Greek, 11
Greener, Richard, 125
Gregory, Sir William, 20
Gurney, Daniel, 127
Gwynne, Rowland, xii

Hackney, Joseph, 90
Hale, Sir Matthew, xiv
Hall, John, 28
Halle, Germany, 1, 70
Hammond, Anthony, xii
Harcourt, Simon, 90
Harding, Thomas, 127
Harle, James, 127
Harper, John, 58
Harrison, Thomas, 126
Hartlib, Samuel, xi, xiii
Harvey
    Jacob, 135
    John, 17
    Mary, 135
Hawkins, Richard, 13–15, 25, 150
Hayns, John, 91
Hayward, Edward, 49
Hearn, Elizabeth, 49
heating, 93, 96, 98
Hebrew, 11
Henderkin, Mary, 61
Heywood
    John, 2, 58, 97
    Richard, 58
Hicks Hall, St. John Street, 90
Hill, Abraham, xii
Hilton
    Joseph, 28
    Mary, 61
Hodgson, William, 127
Holland, 11
Holland, Lady, *see* Rich, Mary
Honnor, Elizabeth, 1
Hope
    Francis, 42, 61
    John, 42, 61
horses, 94; horse bills, 10
houses of correction, xiii–xiv, xxi, 97

housewifery, 107
How, Thomas, 147–8
Howard, William, 148
Hutcheson, Richard, 110
Hutchins, Thomas, 78
Hutton, Richard, workhouse steward, vii–viii, xiv–xvi, xviii, 7, 45, 57, 66, 75, 78, 96, 98, 105–6, 110, 113–14, 118, 120, 122–5, 127, 135, 143, 146; books belonging to, 1; children of, vii; reputation of, 80, 82, 84–5, 88, 99, 104, 115, 143
  Sarah, wife of Richard, vii, 57, 64, 72, 80, 82, 84–6, 88, 97, 104, 106, 114, 116–18, 120, 122, 124–5, 143

Idleness, 95, 104, 106, 113
illness, ix, 8, 54, 56, 62, 72, 74, 80, 84, 97, 111, 113, 121, 131, 145, 154–5; agues, 121; blindness, 72, 131, 144; consumption, 113, 121; convulsions, 72, 121; fever, 113, 121; fits, vii, 72; itch, 121; jaundice, 121; lameness, 72, 131; looseness, 121; rheumatism, 121; smallpox, 121, 155; stranguary, 121
infirmary, proposed, 74; nurses, 54, 72, 74; *see also* medicines
Ingram, Joseph, 126
Institute for Workers Control, ix
Isaac, Sarah, 61
isinglass, 134
Italy, 11

James
  Jonathan, xi
  Richard, 30
Jeffreys, John, 1
Jennings, John, 135, 147–8
Jews, 133
Joans, Elizabeth, 58
Justices of the Peace, 16, 20, 90, 92

Keyford, Somerset, 57
Keith, George, 1
Kight, William, 50, 126
Kingsford, William, 90–1
Kirton, Richard, 13–15, 25
Kitchinman, John, 124
Knolls, John, 104

Labour theory of value, ix, xix
Ladd, William, 102
Lancaster, vii
Latin, 11
Law, John, 90
Lawrence, Mary, 58
Lawson, Thomas, x
Lee
  John, 127
  Mo, 28

Leek, Staffordshire, 62
legacies, viii, xvi–xvii, 13–15, 26–8, 37, 40–1, 46, 49–51, 53, 61, 75, 78, 99, 130, 135, 141; *see also* benefactions
Lindley
  Amor, 42
  Rachael, 42
Little Holland House, 14–15, 27
Locke, John, xii
Lodge, Robert, 132
Lombard Street, vii
Love, John, 61
Luttrell, Narcissus, 90

Mackworth, Humphrey, xii
Maidstone, Kent, xxi
manufacturing *see* employments
Marlow, John, 50
Martin
  Josiah, 125–6
  Thomas, 26
Marx, Karl, viii
Mason, Benjamin, 1, 26, 85
meetings, 152–4; Bull and Mouth monthly meeting, 27, 45, 49; Cork monthly meeting, 38; Devonshire House monthly meeting, 49, 58, 61; Friends' Workhouse monthly meeting, 27; Hammersmith monthly meeting, 13–15, 27; Horsley Down monthly meeting, 49; Meeting of Twelve, viii n.; monthly meetings, viii, x, xiv–xviii, 37, 46, 56, 61, 68, 74, 80, 93, 99, 110, 114, 122–3, 141, 147, 155; Peel monthly meeting, 38, 49, 61, 64, 152–3; quarterly meetings, viii n., xv, 58, 74, 82, 115, 141; Ratcliff monthly meeting, 49; Savoy monthly meeting, 15, 27, 49; Six Weeks meeting, viii n., x, xv; Six Weeks meeting in London, 15, 25, 40; Southwark monthly meeting, 61; women's meeting, viii n., 24, 58, 120; yearly meeting, viii n., xv
medicines, 111–13, 121, 131, 144; anastringent juleps, 111; bezoar powders, 113; bisquits, 111; cheese cake, 111; chocolate, 111–13; cinnamon, 111, 113; claret, 111, 113; coffee, 113; conserve of roses, 111–13; cordials, 113; eggs, 112–13, 144; hart's horn, 111, 113; juleps, 113, 121; ointments, 121; oysters, 111; physic, 111, 121, 156; red cow's milk, 112–13; salve, 121; sugar, 104, 111, 113; wine, 111, 155
Metcalfe, John, 90–1
Middlesex, Justices of the Peace, xiv, 90, 92
Miles, Joane, 58
Miller
  John, 53
  Katherine, 49

Milner, John, 90–1
Mitchell, Doyly, 90–1
Molleson, Gilbert, 110
Montague, William, Lord Chief Justice, 17
mops, 49; mop yarn, xvi, 2–3, 10, 37, 49, 93–6
Morgan, Samuel, 125–6
murder, allegation of, 87

Neat, Anthony, 148
needles, 24
Newton, Hannah, maidservant, 84, 116–18
Norton Folgate, Liberty of, 16

Oaths, 16
Odams, Joshua, 53
Offley, John, 90
orphans, 108
Owen, Robert, viii, xxi

Parents, 23–4, 42, 61, 107, 113, 115–18, 120, 130, 132, 141, 145
Paris
    James, 125–6
    Thomas, 124, 147
Park, James, 132
Parliament, x, xii, xv
Partridge, Richard, 75, 78, 126
Pellett, Richard, 17
penmanship, 11
Pennington Street, 40
Pentlebury, Elizabeth, 40–1
Pittflow, Thomas, 30, 35
Pixley, Thomas, 50
Place, Francis, viii, xxi
Plant, John, 124, 147
play, 94, 96, 155
Pollexfen, John, xii
poor law, xii
poor relief, ix, xxi
Portland, Thomas, 58
Powell, John, xvi n., 97
Priest, Thomas, 58
Prime, John, 17
prisons, x, xiv n.
Pritty, Jacob, 61
privacy, 97
privileges, 45, 97
provisions, 49, 51, 72, 84–8, 97, 99, 106, 128; *see also* bill of fare, diet
Puckridge, Nathaniel, 82
punishments, ix, xiii, 42, 82, 117, 120
Purchas, Arthur, 57

Rand, Elizabeth, 43–5, 58
Read, Joseph, 61
reading, 94, 107–8
reformation of manners, 145
religious matters, memoranda on, 65, 102, 104, 132–3, 140

rents, 37, 49, 50–1, 75–6, 92, 128
Reynolds, Thomas, 147
Rhoades, Thomas, 124, 147–8
Rich, Mary, Lady Holland, countess of Warwick, 15
Richardson
    Richard, 75, 78
    Samuel, 61
Robins
    Richard, 148
    Thomas, 61
Rocque's map of London, xiv
Rosier, Daniel, 58
Rowe, Sir Thomas, xiv, 90, 92
Russell, John, 110, 127

Saffron Walden, Essex, xxi
St. Giles in the Fields, Middlesex, xxi
Salmon
    John, 17
    Robert, 17
Sandon, Thomas, 127
Sands
    Sir Edwin, 133
    Martha, 58
    Thomas, 57, 61
Sanson, W., 61
Saunders, Richard, 110
scales, 84
scholars, xvi
school, 116–17; sewing school, 107
    master, 47, 57, 105, 108, 116, 118, 153; *see also* Elbeck, Henry
    mistress, 23–4, 52, 98, 107–8, 153
Scott, Prince, 28
secret correspondence, xvii, 23
self-help, x
Sessions of the Peace, 90, 92
Sherrwin, Robert, 147
shoe repair, 36
shop maids, 107
Shorey, John, 90–1
Shrimpton, J., 53
Smart, Richard, 58
Smith
    Edward, 17
    Martha, 58
    Thomas, 116–18
Society for Promoting Christian Knowledge, xx
South, William Walker, 125
South Sea stock, 49, 51
Spencer, John, 124
Sprak
    Elizabeth, 67
    Mary, 67
    Samuel, 67
Stafford, 21–2
Stanbury, John, 127
Stanton, Elizabeth, 87

Steel, William, 53
stock, 37, 93
Storrey, Phillip, 110
stow grates, 63, 77
Straham, Dorothy, 58
subscriptions, 37, 50, 51
Sunderland, Elkanah, 30
Swain, James, 127

Table manners, 97
tailoring, vii, 30, 33, 35, 117
tallow chandlers, 93
Tallowfield, William, 62
Tanner, John, 114
taxes, 37, 50–1, 108
Taylor
   Cornelius, 125, 149
   Thomas, 21–2, 28
tenants, 118
Thames Street, 75–6, 78
theft, 8, 84, 152
Thorncombe, Dorset, 67
thread, xvi, 24, 29, 31, 35
threats, of arson, 8
Tillotson, John, Archbishop of Canterbury, 133
tobacco, 97, 152
Toovey, Charles, 2
Townsend, William, vii n., xviii, 77, 80–2, 84–8
Trafford, Samuel, xvi n.
Tuller, John, 90
turpentine, 139
Tuxbury (? Tewkesbury, Gloucestershire), 2

Under-sheriffs, 16
Underwood, Thomas, 127

Vandewall
   Daniel, 90, 92, 124, 127
   John, 124

Vaughan, Rowland, x–xi
Venner, John, 91
vermin, 139
vinegar, 134
visitors, 58, 86, 97

Waite, Thomas, 58
Wall, W., 1
Ward, Alexander, 90–1
Ware, Hertfordshire, 62
Warwick, Lady, *see* Rich, Mary
washing, 23, 54, 72, 97, 153
watch purchased, 63
Webb, Richard, 17
Webster, William, 1
weights, 84, 87–8
Weller, Samuel, xxi
West
   Henery, 104
   John, 125–6
whispering, 23, 47, 80
Whitehead, George, 22
Whiting, John, 124
Wilson, John, 111
Windsor, Dean and Canons of, 76
Wingfield, George, 26, 110, 126
Withers
   Josiah, 128
   Robert, 129
Wood, Edward, 148
Woodstock, Rebecca, 31, 36
wool, 10, 46, 49, 51, 94–5, 123, 130
work *see* employments
workhouse test, xx, xxi
workhouses, vii n., xi–xiv, xx–xxi, 145
Worster, Henry, 40–1
writing, 11, 23, 49, 94, 96, 107–8

Yarmouth, Norfolk, 42
yarn, 94, 96, 128, 129, 130

LONDON RECORD SOCIETY

The London Record Society was founded in December 1964 to publish transcripts, abstracts and lists of the primary sources for the history of London, and generally to stimulate interest in archives relating to London. Membership is open to any individual or institution; the annual subscription is £7 ($15) for individuals and £10 ($23) for institutions, which entitles a member to receive one copy of each volume published during the year and to attend and vote at meetings of the Society. Prospective members should apply to the Hon. Secretary, Miss Heather Creaton, c/o Institute of Historical Research, Senate House, London, WC1E 7HU.

The following volumes have already been published:
1. *London Possessory Assizes: a calendar*, edited by Helena M. Chew (1965)
2. *London Inhabitants within the Walls, 1695*, with an introduction by D. V. Glass (1966)
3. *London Consistory Court Wills, 1492–1547*, edited by Ida Darlington (1967)
4. *Scriveners' Company Common Paper, 1357–1628, with a continuation to 1678*, edited by Francis W. Steer (1968)
5. *London Radicalism, 1830–1843: a selection from the papers of Francis Place*, edited by D. J. Rowe (1970)
6. *The London Eyre of 1244*, edited by Helena M. Chew and Martin Weinbaum (1970)
7. *The Cartulary of Holy Trinity Aldgate*, edited by Gerald A. J. Hodgett (1971)
8. *The Port and Trade of Early Elizabethan London: documents*, edited by Brian Dietz (1972)
9. *The Spanish Company*, by Pauline Croft (1973)
10. *London Assize of Nuisance, 1301–1431: a calendar*, edited by Helena M. Chew and William Kellaway (1973)
11. *Two Calvinistic Methodist Chapels, 1743–1811: the London Tabernacle and Spa Fields Chapel*, edited by Edwin Welch (1975)
12. *The London Eyre of 1276*, edited by Martin Weinbaum (1976)
13. *The Church in London, 1375–1392*, edited by A. K. McHardy (1977)
14. *Committees for Repeal of the Test and Corporation Acts: Minutes, 1786–90 and 1827–8*, edited by Thomas W. Davis (1978)
15. *Joshua Johnson's Letterbox, 1771–4: letters from a merchant in London to his partners in Maryland*, edited by Jacob M. Price (1979)
16. *London and Middlesex Chantry Certificate, 1548*, edited by C. J. Kitching (1980)

17. *London Politics, 1713–1717: Minutes of a Whig Club, 1714–17*, edited by H. Horwitz; *London Pollbooks, 1713*, edited by W. A. Speck and W. A. Gray (1981)
18. *Parish Fraternity Register: fraternity of the Holy Trinity and SS. Fabian and Sebastian in the parish of St Botolph without Aldersgate*, edited by Patricia Basing (1982)
19. *Trinity House of Deptford: Transactions, 1609–35*, edited by G. G. Harris (1983)
20. *Chamber Accounts of the sixteenth century*, edited by Betty R. Masters (1984)
21. *The Letters of John Paige, London merchant, 1648–58*, edited by George F. Steckley (1984)
22. *A Survey of Documentary Sources for Property Holding in London before the Great Fire*, by Derek Keene and Vanessa Harding (1985)
23. *The Commissions for Building Fifty New Churches*, edited by M. H. Port (1986)
24. *Richard Hutton's Complaints Book*, edited by Timothy V. Hitchcock (1987)

All volumes are still in print; apply to Hon. Secretary. Price to individual members £7 ($15) each; to institutional members £10 ($23) each; and to non-members £12 ($28) each.